YOGA
FOR RUNNERS

YOGA FOR RUNNERS

Lexie Williamson

BLOOMSBURY

LONDON • NEW DELHI • NEW YORK • SYDNEY

Published by Bloomsbury Publishing Plc
50 Bedford Square
London WC1B 3DP
www.bloomsbury.com

Bloomsbury is a trademark of Bloomsbury Publishing Plc

First edition 2014

ISBN (print): 978-1-4081-9065-4
ISBN (edpf): 978-1-4081-9067-8
ISBN (epub): 978-1-4081-9066-1

A CIP catalogue record for this book is available from the British Library.

Acknowledgements
Cover photograph © Getty Images
All inside images © John-Paul Bland Photography, (www.jpbland.co.uk) with the exception of the following: pp.173 x 4, 178 and 201 © Getty Images; pp. 6, 8, 18, 38, 53, 72, 109, 112, 115, 138, 140, 142, 172, 176, 181, 182, 197, 198 × 4, 200, 201 and 221 © Shutterstock.com; pp. 22 and 196 © Sandra R. Barba; p. 50 © Juriah Mosin/Shutterstock.com; p. 186 © Rihardzz/Shutterstock.com; pp. 86 and 177 © Rob Wilson; p. 135 © muzsy/Shutterstock.com; p. 168 © Bruno Ismael Silva Alves/Shutterstock.com; p.175 © Pawel Kowalczyk/Shutterstock.com; p.183 © Maxisport/Shutterstock.com; p.191 © FCG/Shutterstock.com; p. 203 © Ostill/Shutterstock.com; p.204 © Lawrence Wee/Shutterstock.com

Commissioning Editor: Lisa Thomas
Editor: Sarah Cole
Design: Rod Teasdale

Typeset in 9.5pt on 13pt Myriad Pro Light by White Rabbit Editions, Barnstaple, Devon.
Printed and bound in China by C&C Offset Printing Co.
10 9 8 7 6 5 4 3 2 1

CONTENTS

ACKNOWLEDGEMENTS

I would like to thank running gait expert Mitchell Phillips, podiatrist Dr Brian Fullem, orthopaedic surgeon Nicholas DiNubile and fellow Yoga Sports Coach™ Anthea Sweet for their valued contributions to Yoga for Runners. I would also like to acknowledge the runners who supplied quotes: Duncan Haughey and Daniel Everall of the Elmbridge Road Runners, and blogger Hannah Dunnell. A huge thank you to my super-fit models Rory Spicer, Sarah Bowen, Sam Bishop and Lindsey Brown who found time in their training and work schedules to provide the visuals. Thank you John-Paul Bland for your superb photography. Finally, a huge thank you to the family Williamson: Cameron, Finlay, Lauren, Skye and my husband Tom.

INTRODUCTION

The idea behind Yoga for Runners, and its cycling counterpart, was to offer practical, sport-specific yoga in the style of a training manual that appealed equally to men and women.

I was keen to get away from the outmoded views that yoga is a) only for women and the super supple, and b) must involve chakras, chanting or tying yourself in impossible pretzel-like knots.

All the models in this book are runners, triathletes or decathletes with realistic levels of flexibility. I have written this book taking into account the hours you spend running. If you have limited range of motion, knee issues or tight hamstrings there is a pose in this book for you.

A huge range of sportspeople, from runners and cyclists, to soccer and tennis stars (think Scott Jurek, Cadel Evans, Ryan Giggs and Andy Murray) include yoga in their strength and conditioning regimes and interest amongst sportspeople is steadily increasing.

The primary reason for this is usually injury avoidance. Yoga is famous, first and foremost, as a stretching discipline. A regular yoga practice can help runners side-step common running injuries like iliotibial band syndrome or plantar fasciitis, especially if accompanied by massage and adequate recovery time.

But as the chapter headings show,

there's a lot more to yoga than ironing out muscular kinks caused by pounding the streets or traversing the trails. Yoga can be used to positively enhance running performance, be it focusing a jittery mind, breathing easier, running taller or even sleeping deeper.

I hope you enjoy exploring the complementary relationship between running and yoga.

Stretching is really just the beginning.

' I took up yoga for flexibility, body awareness and centred focus. '

Scott Jurek, ultrarunning champion,

Eat and Run **(Bloomsbury, 2012)**

This is not a stretching book. It's not a book about breathing techniques, core strength, balance, posture or concentration. *Yoga for Runners* includes all these physical and mental elements of yoga, adapted specifically for runners.

Every single posture and technique is traced back to running performance, from maintaining pace through breathing rhythms to using relaxation to recharge for tomorrow's run.

Running is a fantastic cardiovascular workout that floods the body with feel-good endorphins. Many find its repetitive nature a natural stress reliever.

The downside of this repetitive motion is that it taxes a few select muscle groups (hamstrings, quads, hip flexors and calves) and underuses the rest. Over time this imbalance restricts fluid running form and can trigger the overuse injuries that commonly beset runners.

Yoga addresses this by re-establishing balance. It lengthens muscles, realigns joints and stabilises the body through strengthening postures so the runner is better equipped to cope with the rigours of running.

'Yoga is like pressing the "reset" button for body and mind', explains Duncan Haughey, Chairman of the Elmbridge Road Runners club in Surrey, UK. 'It allows me to be ready to train hard again the next day.'

It is true that for many runners yoga has an injury prevention – or 'prehab' – role. But it can also positively impact running performance in so many ways by improving running posture, aiding proprioception and sharpening the mind.

In this sense yoga is truly a whole-body discipline, addressing the runner from the soles of his feet to the thoughts in his head.

How you use this book will depend on a number of factors:

- the type of running (trail, road, ultra, marathon, etc.)
- the length, frequency and intensity of your training sessions
- individual strengths and weaknesses.

If your core is weak, turn straight to Chapter 7. Do you have tight hips but hate to stretch? Try a dynamic, hip-opening sequence from Chapter 6. Can't sleep? Look at Chapter 11, Recovery Yoga.

Refer to the guide at the end of this chapter for more suggestions about how to select the right techniques and incorporate them into your training schedule.

But first, here is a summary of the top 10 benefits of yoga for runners.

1 Yoga as 'prehab'

Many runners take up yoga after suffering with an injury. But yoga is ideally practised as a form of 'prehab' rather than 'rehab.' This means achieving a 'normal' level of mobility and improving strength, stability, coordination and proprioception to prevent injury. Yoga also creates a heightened body awareness, so runners notice a niggle before it becomes a full-blown injury.

❛ Yoga teaches us body wisdom and awareness. We can respond to the messages the body is sending as it tries to tell us something is wrong. First the body whispers, then the body shouts and eventually the body screams. Yoga lets you hear when the body is whispering. ❜

Julie Hustwayte, chartered physiotherapist
and Yoga Sports Coach™

Starting yoga 1: yoga as cross training

The consensus among running experts is that a runner who only runs courts injury, burnout and even boredom. Cross training is a good way to maintain cardiovascular fitness and keep training fresh. Lower impact examples include swimming and cycling. If you are struggling to justify spending time on yoga, view it simply as a useful cross training session. Also struggling to squeeze in a gym session? Choose a stronger style of yoga, such as ashtanga or power yoga, for both core, leg and upper body strength and flexibility – ticking two boxes in one go.

2 Focus, focus, focus

The difference between a good runner and a great runner is the ability to concentrate. Physical training is so often undermined by the trickery of our own thought processes. The mind has a tendency to wander and conjure up negative thoughts – 'gremlins' – at exactly the wrong point in a run or race. The underlying purpose of yoga is to first tame, then harness the power of the mind. Its concentration techniques are perfect for endurance athletes like runners looking to sharpen mental focus (see Chapter 9).

3 Breathing for endurance

Many elite-level athletes appreciate the power of the breath as a performance tool, rather than a mere automatic function, be they runners or cyclists, golfers or tennis players. Novice runners complain of being 'out of breath' as their body adapts, but as cardiovascular fitness improves the opportunity emerges to experiment with a range of performance-enhancing breathing techniques adapted from yoga. This process begins with simple breath awareness and diaphragmatic (or 'belly') breathing, through to more technical breathing/stride rhythms to maintain pace and mental focus. Finally, those suffering with pre-race nerves can use calming breathing methods. Slow, deep breathing reduces adrenaline levels sufficiently to let the shoulders drop and the mind focus (see Chapter 10).

Starting yoga 2: how to breathe

In yoga jargon, a 'breath' is both an inhalation and an exhalation, rather than just a single breath in. Breathing is slow and deep, so holding a posture for five to ten breaths, as is the instruction for most postures in this book, should take sixty seconds, or longer, depending on your breathing rate. Yoga breathing is also generally deeper and ideally abdominal. Not only is this a more calming way to breathe, it also grounds or stabilises the body, especially in balances. Unless otherwise instructed, always breathe through your nose. This helps engage the parasympathetic nervous system, which calms and focuses the mind. In this state you (a) are less likely to push or strain in postures and (b) start to focus the mind inwards in preparation for meditation. This heightened awareness is especially useful for athletes as they are more likely to notice potential injury or muscular tightness before it becomes an issue. Finally, when moving dynamically from one posture to the next you may be asked to 'synchronise the breath and movement'. This means you might inhale in warrior 2 (page 152) and transition into side angle pose (page 152) on an exhale. The breathing element of yoga can be confusing to start with, and beginners often hold their breath. Once students are familiar and comfortable with the physical postures, this heightened breath awareness becomes automatic. With this additional focus simple stretching is then transformed into the mind/body discipline of yoga.

4 Tension-free running

There are not many sports where the ability to hold tension is an asset. Runners tend to accumulate tension in the jaw, neck and shoulders, as the fast-twitch muscles in these areas respond quickly to stress by rapidly contracting. Tight or hunched shoulders not only hinder relaxed running form by jarring the arm swing, but sap vital energy and inhibit deep breathing. Most of the chapters in *Yoga for Runners* tackle tension through stretching, breathing and relaxation exercises, but for quick 'on-run' techniques to loosen those shoulders turn to Chapter 3.

5 Perfect posture

The subject of form is much debated, but most schools of running agree on the principle of 'running tall' with an upright, yet relaxed posture. It aids deep breathing, prevents injury and looks so much better than hunched shuffling. Yet many of us lack good everyday posture, especially when work requires us to sit at a desk for eight hours a day. A good first yoga lesson begins with the seemingly simple, yet crucial role of correct standing posture. 'Don't run before you can stand' is the mantra. Chapter 2 explores everyday posture, and then ideal running form with the help of a running gait expert.

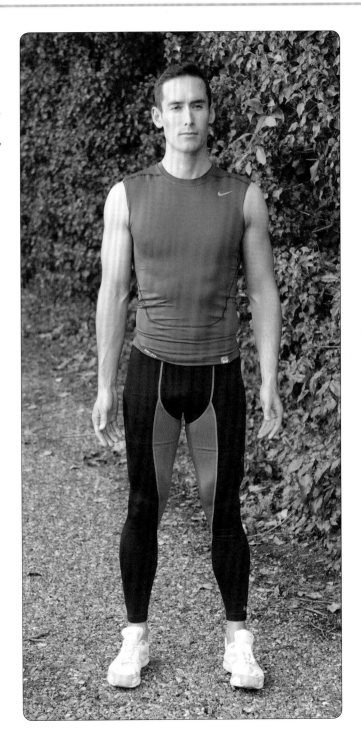

Starting yoga 3: the right class for runners

There are as many types of yoga as there are martial arts, so it's worth doing a little research. If you are training intensively or have injuries opt for a gentle class with a focus on deep stretching like hatha yoga. To build strength and stretch look for dynamic styles like power yoga, vinyasa flow or ashtanga. Here's a guide to the main types and their relevance for runners:

1 **Hot yoga** (105°F with 35 per cent humidity) is popular with runners looking to either lose weight or gain flexibility. A hot yoga session also releases feel-good hormones, similar to the runner's 'high'. While it's true that sweltering heat aids stretching be careful not to push beyond your natural range of motion. Finally, drink as if you were running the Marathon de Sables to stay hydrated. Search online for Bikram or hot yoga to find a local studio.

2 **Ashtanga** is a strenuous style of yoga, and follows the same pattern of postures or 'series' becoming progressively more advanced as you gain experience. There's an emphasis on upper body strength, with lots of plank and downward facing dog. The former is great for building overall core strength, but many runners struggle with dog due to tight hamstrings. Athletes generally love the faster pace and competitive element of ashtanga.

3 **Power yoga** is worth trying if you are struggling to fit in both a yoga session and a gym session. It builds strength using just the body weight. Power yoga is similar to ashtanga, but the content may change from session to session. It tends to be popular with men because of its challenging nature, but there is less

6 Balance and proprioception

Yoga is uniquely placed to improve a runner's overall sense of balance and, especially proprioception, or the body's ability to sense the location of its limbs in space. The latter is a skill vital for hill or trail runners, who are required to rapidly assess uneven ground or leap from rock to rock. But balances are equally useful for the city pavement runner. They reinforce the muscles of the feet, ankles and lower leg, equipping the runner to better absorb the impact of training on a hard surface. Finally, as yoga balances are always performed barefoot, they hold a unique appeal for those thinking of switching to barefoot running by improving the strength

and responsiveness of the feet. See Chapter 4 on balance training and Chapter 5 on stretches for the feet, ankles and lower legs.

emphasis on the mental side of yoga. Like ashtanga, this is a style to avoid if you are burnt out from training, very stiff or injured.

4   **Vinyasa flow** is a good choice for runners. This style of yoga flows (moves from posture to posture rather than holding statically), but is not too strenuous. This makes it ideal for runners bored by static stretching but not bendy or strong enough to brave power or ashtanga yoga. It may also be named dynamic yoga.

5   **Hatha yoga** is the gentlest style of yoga. Hatha will probably be a slower class with more static postures and an emphasis on the mental side of yoga. A session will include breathing exercises, meditation or relaxation. Hatha is a great option if you are training hard and need to simply stretch and unwind.

6   **Iyengar yoga** involves holding poses statically for longer periods of time (which can be just as tough as fast-flowing yoga), often using props such as blocks and straps. There is an emphasis on precision and alignment, which is good for athletes. However, this static style of yoga requires patience, so if you dislike static stretching opt for a flowing style.

7   **Yoga for runners** – if you are lucky enough to have a yoga for runners class nearby, do attend. The content will be tailored specifically to you. The instructor will also be familiar with runner's bodies, sympathetic to the rigours of training and have a basic knowledge of common running injuries. At least half (and often more) of the class are likely to be male, and the language will be more 'muscles and performance' than 'chakras and Sanskrit'.

Starting yoga 4: yoga jargon

Yoga, just like running, has its own jargon. Here are some common terms you will hear in a class, with a brief explanation.

Tail bone – The sacrum, or wedge-shaped bone at the base of the spine.
Heart centre – The area around the middle of the chest.
Sit bones – The ischial tuberosities, or two bony protrusions on the base of the pelvis.
Namaste – An Indian greeting accompanied by placing the palms together in a prayer position and bowing the head. This usually signifies the end of the class.

7 Strengthening the core

Many runners are sent to yoga or Pilates by a physiotherapist to strengthen the core, and rightly so. The core (meaning not just the abdominals, but hip flexors, gluteals and lower back) is central to both disciplines. All the standing postures, including the balances heavily recruit the core, sometimes using the body weight to challenge it further. The triangle pose, for example, tips the entire upper body into a side-bend, forcing the side abdominals, or obliques, into a stabilising role. Yoga also has a range of 'pure' core postures, like plank, that are vital for running posture, power and injury prevention. Where possible, *Yoga for Runners* has tweaked these techniques to create more running-specific movements. See Chapter 7 for more on the core.

Starting yoga 4: running-specific yoga

Runner's strength and conditioning techniques should be 'functional', which essentially means training the same muscles you use to clock up the miles on the road, or ascend the hills. I have tried to adapt as many yoga techniques as possible to make them running-specific. Some are naturally functional. Lunges like warrior 1 (page 148), for instance, mimic a wide stride. Running plank 1 (page 124) requires the runner to hold the torso still and stable while lifting the legs, replicating a running movement. All-fours core techniques raise the right leg and left arm just as we do when walking and running. Finally, runners can re-create a running motion, then bring in balance, coordination and core stability by rising onto the ball of the standing foot as the leg swings through (see the stride sequences in Chapter 4, page 64).

8 Strength without bulk

Yoga is often classed as a stretching discipline, but newcomers are often surprised at the intensity of holding, say, side angle pose for more than a minute. Muscles quiver, foreheads glisten with sweat and jaws clench! Unlike gym-based weight machines that tend to isolate muscle groups, the entire body is engaged in holding the pose: feet, legs, core, back, shoulders and arms. Even the breathing is slowed and regulated while the mind focuses on balancing. This whole-body approach reduces the chance of creating muscular imbalances through strength work. Muscles also contract eccentrically (stretch as they contract) to create long, lean fibres, ideal for runners who want to stay light on their feet.

9 Finding 'flow'

❛ The similarities between yoga and flow are extremely strong; in fact it makes sense to think of yoga as a very thoroughly planned flow activity. ❜

Mihaly Csikszentmihalyi, Flow (1992, Harper & Row)

Csikszentmihalyi has also described flow (or 'the zone') as being 100 per cent absorbed in the task at hand. Runners have reported varying states of the zone, but total concentration is the 'critical component', according to Csikszentmihalyi. Every aspect of yoga, from the physical postures to the breathing techniques and, finally, meditation, is designed to re-create this state of concentration, or what yogis call 'one-pointedness'. Experiment with some concentration exercises in Chapter 9.

10 Optimising recovery

To some runners 'recovery' is simply time not running. Others relax in front of a movie or book a massage. From a yoga viewpoint, proper recovery means resting both physically and mentally. Movie watching is an enjoyable distraction, but the mind is still stimulated. Long-held restorative stretches, as well as breathing, relaxation and meditation, tease out physical tension and calm the mind. These wind down techniques pave the way for the oldest and best recovery technique of all: a good night's sleep.

INCORPORATING YOGA INTO TRAINING

Yoga is highly versatile; a practice might range from a post-run, deep static hamstring stretch to a gymnastic, energetic flow to build strength. It is useful to know how to tailor your yoga to balance the intensity of the run. A common-sense rule is the higher the intensity of the run or frequency of training sessions, the gentler the yoga.

If you're training hard concentrate on restoring muscles to their resting length to avoid injury and maintain balance. Avoid strong yoga that may deplete your energy levels further. Focus particularly on your feet, legs, hips and glutes, using a simple sequence like the post-run strap sequence from Chapter 6 (page 110), which requires little thought or planning, and therefore becomes an integral part of your post-run ritual. Invert your legs by lying on the floor and looping a strap around the soles of your feet.

If you have an off-season, or are training at a lower intensity, power up your yoga sessions by holding strengthening postures or exploring a fast-moving, dynamic sequence. Try the runner's sun salutation (page 156) and mix in running variations of running planks from Chapter 7. Join a power yoga or ashtanga class. Use this time to experiment with techniques to improve breathing efficiency or mental clarity to give you the edge when returning to running or competing.

Tailor post-run yoga to balance the intensity of the session. Here are some suggestions:

1 **Hill reps or sprints** – Static hamstring, quad, glute and hip flexor stretches, such as runner's lunge (page 98), walking dog (page 82), figure four (page 104), and side-bends like triangle (page 153).

2 **Long road or trail run** – Foot stretches, leg elevations like legs up the wall (page 211), full body stretches to decompress the back, and gentle hip mobilising movements like the post-run hip sequence (page 108) or post-run lunge sequence (page 98). If the endorphins are still pumping at bedtime try deep breathing, meditation or relaxation techniques.

3 **Light run** – A dynamic cool-down, such as the runner's sun salutation (page 156), with extra core work in plank (page 122). Balances such as tree pose (page 58). Stronger standing postures like the lunging warrior 1 (page 148) and triangle.

4 **Rest days** – A stronger dynamic sequence to build power in the quads and glutes, such as the leg power flow sequence (page 160). Add in some lateral strengthening postures to restore muscle imbalances from running. Alternatively use yoga's many meditation and relaxation techniques to optimise recovery and enjoy a total physical and mental break from training.

Stretching: pre- or post-run?

The short answer is 'post-run'. Statically stretching cold, tight muscles beforehand could lead to muscle strains and tears. Instead do a warm-up comprising specific, low-impact moves to get the blood flowing to running muscle groups (see tension-release warm-up, page 45). This could include marching, leg swings and 'back kicks' to warm up the quads. These can either be done on the spot or dynamically as plyometric stretches by jumping from foot to foot. The walking lunge movement is also a  fantastic warm-up for runners (see walking lunge warm-up, page 69). Immediately after a run is the perfect time to stretch either statically or dynamically when the muscles are warm and pliable. The idea is not to become super supple – runners don't need the flexibility of dancers – but to maintain a good range of motion and hone in on problem areas such as tight calves or quads to stay running and injury-free.

02

❛ If it's true to say 'you are what you eat' then it's equally fair to say 'you run like you stand'. ❜

Mitchell Phillips, director, Stride UK

The term 'running tall' denotes an upright, yet relaxed running stance – a feeling of lengthening without rigidity. This ideal posture encourages deeper breathing, creates a softer, lighter footfall, and reduces the chance of discomfort and injury brought on by slouching.

But before you can run tall, or even walk tall, it's necessary to learn how to stand. Yoga's mountain pose is designed to iron out the kinks in everyday standing posture, from the toes to the crown of the head. Practising it regularly will ensure that no bad postural habits are transferred onto the run.

The lift and lengthen sequence in this chapter explores variations of mountain pose to both decompress your spine and stretch your torso. The sitting tall sequence is for runners with sedentary jobs who don't want the 9–5 to impact on posture. It offers office-based hip flexor, glute and back stretches.

The next step is to reinforce your torso through core strengthening postures to create a stable, central pillar, and then stretch the chest and draw back the shoulders through a series of upper body strap stretches.

Finally, we examine ideal running posture with help from a gait expert who guides us through the dos and don'ts of running form, and offers the memorable mantra: 'Head in line, neutral spine'.

CORRECT RUNNING POSTURE

The correct running posture has the following benefits.

1 REDUCES INJURIES

Take poor posture on a run and you risk injury, especially as the miles mount up and the body fatigues and slumps further. A curved spine will strain the muscles of the lower back and shoulders, and shift the weight forwards stressing the knees, shins and Achilles. This is exacerbated if you run looking down at your feet or the path instead of straight ahead.

2 CREATES A FASTER, LIGHTER STRIDE

The average head weighs 10 pounds (around 4.5 kg). If the spine is rounded and the head juts forwards, it not only strains the neck and upper back muscles but creates a slow, heavy footfall and shortens the stride. An audible pounding sound is often a sign of poor posture. Realign your body, stacking your head over your shoulders and shoulders over hips to lighten your step and pick up speed.

3 AIDS DEEPER BREATHING

Rounded shoulders and spine compress the front of the body, making it harder to take a deep, full breath, just when the muscles need oxygen most. A simple way to assess the impact of slouching on breathing is to take this quick slouch test. Deliberately slump forwards, letting your back and shoulders become round and your head drop lower. Take a couple of breaths and notice how restricted and short the respiration has become. Now rise up, ease your shoulders back, gaze forwards and repeat the experiment. Notice how the abdomen and ribcage are free to expand. Runners often slump in the latter stages of a race, but that extra oxygen will make all the difference to tired muscles.

4 BOOSTS CONFIDENCE

Drawing yourself upwards to your full height provides a positive psychological boost. It's common for the mind to become negative as the body tires during racing, and start to question ability and training. This negative mode of thinking causes the head to drop both literally and psychologically. Break this circle of negativity by raising the head and drawing back the shoulders to create a posture that shouts: 'I can do this!'

STANDING TALL

The first stage of running tall is learning how to stand. The body should be upright, but not stiff. It should be perfectly balanced, with the weight equally placed on the feet and the head stacked over the shoulders. In yoga, proper alignment in a standing position is learned through practising mountain pose, or tadasana. These basic lessons in how to stand will create a natural postural awareness that will benefit running form.

1 Wall posture check

A physiotherapist can conduct a detailed postural assessment, which is well worth the investment, but a simple, quick way to gauge posture is to rest the back against the wall. Start by placing your feet hip-width apart, heels in contact with the surface. Then lightly rest your bottom and back of the head on the wall, tucking the chin slightly in. How does it feel: natural or artificially upright? Are the tops of your shoulders against the wall or peeling away from its surface? Can you draw them back so they press into the wall? Does your head feel too far back? Now step away from the wall, but maintain this newfound posture and see how it feels to truly stand tall. Replicate this feeling of lift and length when you next run.

2 Mountain pose

At a glance mountain pose might look easy. Don't be fooled: there's more to this posture than standing still. It is the blueprint for yoga's standing postures. Mountain aligns the body from the soles of the feet to the top of the head, ensuring it is perfectly balanced before moving on to more complex poses.

Perform it while standing chatting or waiting in a queue and the body will quickly pick up the various cues for standing correctly and do so automatically. Many of these cues are identical to those running coaches and gait experts yell at their runners to encourage good form, so take mountain

ABOVE: *Mountain pose*

pose principles on a run to feel a newfound length and lightness of stride.

Feet: Lift your toes off the floor, splay them wide and lay them down again. Lift the arches of your feet. Spread your weight evenly across the four corners of the feet – little toe, big toe, inner heel and outer heel.

Legs: Engage your leg muscles, feeling the body lifting subtly from the ground upwards.

Pelvis: Tuck the sacrum, or tailbone, slightly under so your pelvis is in 'neutral' – not tipping forwards or back.

Abdomen: Draw your abdomen slightly inwards to lightly engage your muscles without constricting your breathing.

Chest: Lift your sternum to open and elevate your chest.

Shoulders: Draw your shoulders back. Flatten your shoulder blades into your back and slide them downwards.

Head: Balance your head over the centre of your pelvis. Tuck your chin slightly inwards. Lift from the crown of your head. Relax the muscles of your face and jaw. Visualise a plumb line dropping from the crown of your head and landing in between the feet.

Eyes: Gaze straight ahead, or close your eyes and feel your body weight shifting to establish equilibrium.

Breath: Breathe slowly through your nose. Let the breath flow smoothly. Notice the natural pauses during respiration, or listen to the subtle sound of your breathing.

Arms: Rotate your hands to face forwards to open your shoulders. Keep your shoulders still and let your palms rotate back to face the sides. Relax your arms from shoulders to fingertips.

What is the 'neutral spine?'

The shape of the back, with its natural curves, is perfectly designed to absorb the impact of walking and running. Both slouching and over-extending the spine's curves by, say, sticking your bottom out (an anterior pelvic tilt) interferes with this natural alignment. The result is muscular imbalances and a range of knock-on issues, from neck or lower backache to knee injuries. Holding the spine 'in neutral' means maintaining the spine's natural curves. Neutral spine can be found by lying on your back. Bend your legs and place your feet on the floor, hip-distance apart, with your arms resting by your sides. Now perform some pelvic tilts: lift your belly button to the ceiling to exaggerate the lower back curve and flatten the belly button into the floor to eradicate this curve completely. Somewhere in between these two movements lies the neutral spine, usually seen as a small arch just visible in the lumbar, or lower back. This process can also be done standing, by tilting your pelvis forwards and back. The only drawback to this method is that (a) your spine is continually moving and adapting to your body's position, and (b) some people naturally have more of a lumbar curve than others, so their 'neutral' is different. A more useful exercise may be to simply lift from the crown of your head allowing your spine to naturally settle into a neutral position. Repeat this process of lengthening to find your neutral spine while running using one of the many techniques in this chapter such as run tall breathing or puppet string visualisation (see pages 37 and 29).

Tall building visualisation

To encourage an upright running stance imagine that you have a pulley attached to your sternum or breastbone. Fastened to this pulley is a rope the other end of which is fastened to the top of a building a block away. The rope is drawing you towards the building – an image that will both encourage a natural lift in your chest and supply the mental boost needed to propel you forwards when mind and body are flagging. This visualisation was invented by the legendary New Zealand running coach Arthur Lydiard, who helped popularise the concept of running tall.

Lift and lengthen sequence

'Stand straight, shoulders back' is the mantra for this series of standing postures based on mountain pose. But banish any images of a stiff sergeant major stance. The aim is to gain postural awareness and a feeling of height by lengthening your spine without rigidity. The backbend gently opens your chest while the side-bends work the stabilising oblique abdominals.

Stand with your feet hip-distance apart. Hold each pose for five slow breaths.

1 **Mountain pose:** Stand tall. Hold your arms a little way from your sides and turn your palms to face front to open your shoulders. Tuck your chin slightly in and gaze ahead.

2 **Standing backbend:** Tuck your pelvis under, draw your abdomen in and sweep your arms wide, spreading your fingers. Slowly extend your spine into a comfortable backbend. Raise your chin a little. Draw your hands just out of your line of vision.

3 Full body stretch: Return to mountain pose and raise your arms up overhead, interlacing your fingers and turning your palms to face the ceiling. Keep your shoulders low.

4 Standing side-bend (right): On an exhalation tip to the right side trying not to lean forwards or back.

5 Full body stretch: Return to the centre.

6 Standing side-bend (left): On an exhalation tip to the left side trying not to lean forwards or back.

Puppet string visualisation

A simple but powerful way to grow vertically is to imagine that you have a puppet string or thread attached to the crown of your head. This string pulls your head gently upwards and where your head moves the rest of your body follows: your spine lengthens, your torso slides back to stack over your hips and your shoulders release back and down. Picture your puppet string while standing, walking and running.

7 **Shoulder stretch:** Interlace your hands behind your back and roll your shoulders up, back and down. To move deeper, raise your hands up away from your lower back.

Strong and straight sequence

A strong core creates a corset-like effect, enabling your torso to support your spine and remain stable while your legs move freely during running. To really reinforce your core for improved posture and power you need to train your glutes and back as well as your abs. This sequence uses plank, side plank and locust pose to splint the front, sides and back of your torso. Read the plank rules in Chapter 7 (page 123) for guidelines on correct alignment in plank and modifying the pose if you lack abdominal strength or have wrist weakness.

Hold each pose for five to ten breaths.

1 **Forearm plank:** Lower onto your forearms, stacking your elbows under your shoulders. You can make fists with your hands and keep them parallel or interlock them to create a V shape.

2 Forearm side plank: Shift onto your right side and stack your feet on top of each other as if standing. Position your elbow under your shoulder and spread your fingers. Place your top arm by your side to add weight.

3 Pulsing side plank: Stay in side plank, but lift your hips a little on the inhalation and lower as you exhale. Repeat four times.

4 Locust legs: Return to plank and lower to the floor. Move your arms tight to the sides, palms face down and rest your forehead on the floor. On an inhalation raise your right leg off the floor, exhale and lower. Repeat, moving from leg to leg.

5 Full locust: Move your arms away from the sides. On an inhalation lift your legs and upper body off the floor but remain gazing downwards. Spread your fingers.

6 Snake: Repeat locust, but interlace your hands behind your back.

7 Extended child: Lower your knees to the floor and slowly sit back on your heels. Walk your fingertips further forwards to really stretch your shoulders and lower back. Sit up, make fists with your hands and slowly rotate.

Shoulders back sequence

Rounded shoulders create ragged running form. A curved back inhibits deep breathing and shifts your weight forwards. Roll back your shoulders to stretch your 'pecs' and release upper body tension with this series of strap stretches. You will need a cotton yoga belt, or substitute a rubber resistance band, dressing gown cord or old tie.

Stand with your feet hip-distance apart. Hold the strap with your hands a good shoulder-width (wider if your shoulders are tight) apart, palms face down. Draw your abdomen in and tuck your pelvis under.

1 **Warm-up:** Hold the strap loosely. Inhale and sweep your arms up until the strap is roughly overhead. Exhale and return your arms. Repeat four times.

2 **Pectoralis stretch:** Inhale and bend your arms into right angles. Remain here breathing steadily drawing your elbows gradually back. Tuck your pelvis under. Gaze ahead. Stay for five breaths.

3 **Deltoid stretch:**
Take the strap behind you, hands shoulder-width and palms facing forwards. Inhale, and on an exhale, bend your knees deeply and tip into a forward-bend. Stay for five breaths. To exit, drop your hands to your lower back, draw your abdomen in and rise up with a straight back.

4 **Triceps stretch:**
Lay the strap on your right shoulder. Sweep your right arm up and drop it behind your upper back between your shoulder blades. Take your left arm back and aim to interlock your hands. If you cannot make contact, hold both parts of the strap and walk your hands closer. Stay for five breaths. Repeat on the other side.

Brace yourself

Ease your shoulders back with a simple, homemade postural brace. All you need is a long cotton yoga strap. This gentle brace can be worn while sitting at your desk to avoid slumping or while walking around the house. Ensure the brace is loose enough to move freely and breathe deeply.

1 Lay the middle of the strap behind your back so it lies at the bottom of your shoulder blades. Ensure you have an equal length of strap on both sides.

2 Throw both ends of the strap over your shoulders so they hang down the back.

3 Cross the straps so they form an X in the middle of your back.

4 Hold the ends and gently pull down to tighten the brace. Feel your shoulder blades flatten to your back and slide down.

5 Secure the ends of the strap around your waist, but not so tight that it restricts respiration (take a deep abdominal breath in to test). This brace should serve as a reminder to sit, stand or run tall.

SITTING TALL

Hours hunched over a desk driving or spent slouching on the sofa, can take its toll on your posture, and create tight hip flexors, glutes and hamstrings. Perform these four desk-based stretches a few times a day to ensure that a sedentary job won't impact on running form.

Take five breaths in each stretch.

1 **Upper back stretch:** Keep your palms interlaced but drop them down to chest height and rotate them to face inwards. Round your back and tuck your chin in.

2 **Chair backbend:** Swing your arms around the rear base of your chair and hold on. Lift your chest and draw your shoulders back. Raise your chin slightly to open the front of your body.

3 Hamstring/back releaser:
Stand behind the chair, with both hands resting on the top, shoulder-width apart. Your feet should be hip-distance apart. As you exhale fold forwards, making a 90° angle with your body. Bend your knees and rise up gradually.

4 Hip flexor chair stretch: Stand in front of the chair and step your right foot on the seat. Place your hands on your hips, tuck your pelvis under and lean slightly back to feel a stretch at the top of your left leg. Switch legs.

Sit tall at work

- Position the top of the computer monitor at eye level.
- Get up every 15 minutes to walk around or stretch.
- Don't sit with your legs crossed.
- Hold standing-only meetings.
- Use a hands-free headset or speakerphone instead of cradling the phone under one ear.
- Position your feet flat on the floor, using a footrest if necessary.
- Relax your shoulders. Position the spine in 'neutral' (see Box 'What is Neutral Spine?')

RUNNING TALL

'You run like you stand'

Mitchell Phillips, performance analyst and director of the video gait analysis company Stride UK, has said that 'If it's true that "you are what you eat", then it's fair to say "you run like you stand".'

According to Phillips, observing a client standing is a great way to spot imbalances even before they begin to place one foot in front of the other on the treadmill during gait analysis.

'Look at your feet placement – are they sticking out or pointing in?' asks Phillips. 'Is your pelvis tilted forwards creating a deeper curve in the lower lumbar? Are your arms sitting equally and neutrally positioned in line with your ears? Are your hands rotated in, knuckles pointing forwards? All these are tell-tale signs of muscular imbalance.'

'Good' running posture is hard to define. Different schools appear to offer conflicting advice – for example, should you run with an upright spine, or tilt forwards from the ankles with a straight back as the ChiRunners do? The professionals also occasionally break the rules – like Paula Radcliffe with her famous head nod. But according to Phillips, there are some basic postural adjustments that everyone should make:

1 **Lengthen the spine** – or run tall. Run with a lengthened spine and the head and shoulders in line. The internal direction of running is up and the external direction of running is forwards. This upward tendency produces a lightness in the body which means the legs do not have to work so hard to move you forwards. Think of the body suspended by the head and ears with the shoulders and spine simply following suit.

2 **Don't swing your arms across your torso** – this creates a wasteful rotating movement, shifting your body out of its ideal sagittal, or forwards plane of motion. Your legs and arms should be performing in a forward, flexed position. Any movement across or away from your body is burning energy.

3 **Don't hunch your shoulders** – this creates energy-sapping tension and stops your arms swinging freely affecting overall form.

4 **Gaze at least 50 metres in front of you** – allowing your eyeline to drop down causes tightness across your upper back and restricts breathing. Running with a lengthened spine and poised head will also encourage balance and reduces 'heavy' running.

5 **If leaning, lean with your whole body** – I suggest to some runners to lean forwards to help use their body weight to their advantage. It's important not to misinterpret this and lean from the back. The lean should always come from the whole body – tilting forwards until gravity almost sends you over.

Poor posture: rounded shoulders, looking downwards

Improved posture: running tall, looking ahead

Run tall breathing

To both lengthen your spine and loosen your shoulders mid-run try this simple technique, which has a third benefit of slowing and deepening your breathing. As you inhale, imagine you are breathing up the front of the body, from the feet to the crown of the head. Feel the body instinctively lengthen and extend upwards.

As you exhale, visualise breathing down the back of the body and simultaneously relax your shoulders and slide your shoulder blades down the back. Repeat it at every mile marker during a race, to maintain an upright, yet relaxed posture, and/or use it the moment you feel your body tiring and sagging.

RELAXATION IN MOTION

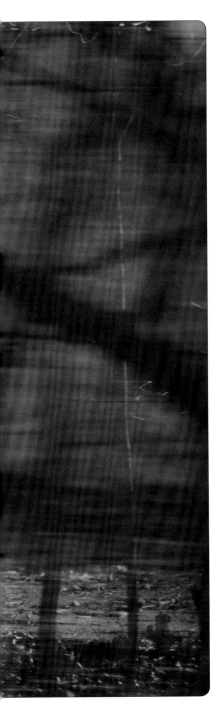

Grimacing, jaw-clenching, fist-squeezing and shoulder-hunching are common sights among runners, especially on race day when the adrenaline is pumping.

These areas of the body are quick to tense up, but tension saps precious energy, often when you need it most. Tightness in the upper body also impacts on overall form by creating a jarring effect that constricts the free flowing movement of the arms and legs.

Banish pre-run stress with a loosening warm-up routine to keep the limbs relaxed. Hone in on tension hot spots like the neck and shoulders, and monitor stress levels mid-run by scanning the body, from fingertips to toes.

TENSION HOT SPOTS

The jaw

Runners often grit their teeth when the going gets tough. The area around the jaw is one of the first to tense up in stressful situations; notice how we clench our teeth when feeling angry or anxious.

To relax your jaw, open your mouth extra wide to mimic a large yawn. Hold for a few seconds, then release. If your jaw is really tight massage it first with your fingertips using small circular motions and then repeat the yawning exercise. Finally, try deliberately clenching your jaw and hold for a few seconds, before releasing.

The neck

Simple slow motion head rolling has a dramatic effect on stress levels. If you suffer from pre-race nerves, or simply need to shed a little upper body tightness, take a moment to perform the following four neck stretches:

1 **Slow motion rolls:** Drop your head down so that your chin tucks in and, in slow motion, roll your head in a semi-circle around to your right shoulder. Lower your right ear to your right shoulder and pause here for five breaths. Repeat, working your way around to your left shoulder. Never tip your head back. Repeat frequently on the train or at your desk. Try closing your eyes and imagining each individual neck muscle stretching in turn.

2 **Lateral stretch:** After performing a few slow motion rolls pause with your head tilted to the right side. Sweep your right arm up and place your palm gently onto your head to ease it deeper into the side stretch. Stay for five breaths. Deepen the stretch by lowering your left shoulder and play with straightening your left arm and moving it a little behind you. Repeat on your left side.

3 **Head rotations:** Lift head so you are gazing straight ahead. Inhale, and as you exhale, turn your head to look over one shoulder, keeping your chin level. Stay for five breaths and repeat on the other side.

4 **Neck release:** Stand tall. Interlace your hands behind the base of your head. Breathe in, and as you breathe out, let the head tip down so your chin tucks in and elbows fall forwards. Keep your back straight. Take a few breaths, then allow your upper back to round and repeat.

The shoulders

Have you ever noticed how your shoulders creep up during the working day often leading to soreness or even muscle cramp? Poor posture, hours spent hunched over a desk or talking with a phone clamped under one ear can all add to shoulder tension. Take this on a run and you will prevent your arms swinging freely and affect the 'mood' of your entire body.

1 Double shoulder rolls: Drop your hands onto the tops of your shoulders. Make slow circles with your elbows.

2 Single shoulder rolls: Take your hands behind your back and clasp your elbows. Roll your right shoulder first, focusing on making smooth circles. Notice any knots or areas of resistance. Switch shoulders.

3 Arm sweeps: Take your arms by your sides and, keeping them straight, sweep them forwards and up on an inhalation and back and down on an exhalation in a wide circular motion. To really expel tension take a deep breath in through the nose as you sweep up and blow the exhale slowly out of your mouth on the downwards movement.

4 Shoulder wrap: Inhale and take your arms wide. As you exhale cross your right arm over your left and wrap your arms tightly in a hug. Tuck your chin in and round your back. Stay for five breaths. Release and take your arms wide. Repeat, crossing left arm over right.

6 Shoulder release: Stand with your feet hip-distance apart and interlace your fingers behind your back. Inhale and lift your chest. Exhale, bend your knees deeply and tip into a forward-bend while raising your arms over your lower back. Relax your head and stay for five, or more, breaths. If your hamstrings are tight, bend your knees further and rest your abdomen on your thighs to concentrate on the shoulder stretch. To exit, drop your hands to your lower back, draw your abdomen in and rise up with a straight back. If this is uncomfortable, try the stretch using a strap.

5 'Eagle' arms: This yoga pose advances the shoulder wrap and is like giving yourself a deep back/shoulder massage. It targets your shoulders, neck extensors and hard-to-reach area around your shoulder blades. As before, inhale and take your arms wide. As you exhale cross your right arm over your left, then bring your palms together. Remain looking ahead. Stay for five or more breaths. Repeat by crossing your left arm over your right.

The hands

To experience how clenching your fists affects arm swing stand up, make a 90° shape with your arms and clench your fists tightly. Now swing your arms as if running. Notice how this immediately restricts your arm movement and tightens the muscles of your shoulders and upper back. Repeat. This time soften your hands, letting your first finger rest lightly on your thumb. Running coaches over the years have devised ingenious ways of encouraging runners to relax their hands. Some advocate imagining they are holding a delicate butterfly, while one coach gave his athletes crisps (potato chips) and checked they were still intact between their finger and thumb at the end of the run.

Let off steam

Deep breathing is a quick and effective way to ease an anxious mind and soften tight muscles. This part-visualisation, part-breathing technique can be performed while running to literally 'let off steam'.

Simply inhale through your nose, purse your lips and release your exhalation slowly through your mouth as if blowing out through a narrow straw. Visualise this slow exhalation as tension leaving your body in a cloud of steam which disperses into the air and disappears. This relaxing technique has the added advantage of slowing down your exhalation which kick-starts a naturally deeper breathing rhythm. For more 'on-run' breathing techniques see Chapter 9.

TENSION RELEASE WARM-UP

Put your tension-releasing techniques together in a feet-to-fingertips warm-up. These broad sweeping movements will serve both to increase blood flow to running muscle groups and shake out any tension, creating a feeling of relaxed looseness.

1 Ankle rolls: Place your hands on your hips. Stand on one leg and lift your other foot off the floor. Rotate your foot to loosen the ankle joint.

2 Leg swings: Relax your arms by your sides and swing your leg back and forth keeping a small bend in the swinging leg. Let your arms swing freely in opposition to mimic the running action.

3 Hip rotations: Place your hands back on your hips and make large smooth circles, keeping your knees soft.

4 Heel taps: Lift your right leg, bend it and turn your knee out. Tap your heel with your left hand and switch sides. Move from side to side keeping your breathing relaxed.

5 Back kicks: Bend your right leg as if taking your heel up to your backside. Switch from side to side, placing your hands on your hips, or letting your arms swing as you march.

6 Relaxed twist: Release your arms and bend your knees more deeply. Twist to the right, allowing your head to turn as well and let your arms swing round. Repeat, rotating from side to side. Let your arms flail.

7 Steam releasers: Sweep both arms up, taking a deep breath in through your nose. As you sweep your arms back and down in a wide circular movement let your exhalation escape like steam through your mouth. Make an audible sighing sound. Visualise tension dispersing with your breath.

8 Water flicks: End by encouraging a looseness in your hands and wrists which are a good indicator of tension levels. Imagine you have water droplets on the tips of your fingers and flick them off.

RELAXATION IN MOTION

Try these on-run head-to-toe techniques to experience true relaxation in motion.

Head: Lower your gaze, not your head. As noted earlier, the average head weighs 10 pounds (4.5 kg), so running with it dropped forwards places stress on your shoulders and upper back.

Mind: What are you thinking? Negative thoughts and self-doubt trigger muscular tension. Pick a mantra from Chapter 9, like 'relax and flow', and repeat until those shoulders drop.

Breath: Link your footfall and breath to create a relaxing rhythm or purse your lips and blow out a long exhalation visualising lactic acid and tension leaving your body like steam.

Shoulders: Think 'low and loose.' Check in regularly with your shoulders as tight ones inhibit a free arm swing and have a knock-on effect, tensing up the whole body. Roll or shrug your shoulders.

Hands: Unclench your fists and flick your fingers as if shaking off water droplets. Then let them curl naturally back into your palm. Relax your thumbs and rest them lightly on top of your first fingers.

Arms: Maintain a 90° angle and allow your arms to swing freely back and forth, but not across your body as this rotates the torso, wasting energy. Periodically release your arms, letting them dangle by your sides and shake out tension.

Legs: Let your lower leg dangle below your knee when you swing your leg through, relaxing your ankle when your foot is in the air. This encourages a natural, fluid stride.

Combatting race day nerves

If you suffer with nerves on race day, dedicate a few minutes to deep breathing. Slow breathing through your nose will reduce adrenaline levels just enough for you to gather your thoughts and re-focus on race strategy. Find a spot away from fellow competitors and sit tall with your eyes closed. Then try one of the following calming techniques breathing solely through the nose.

- Count 1, 2, 3 as you breathe in and 1, 2, 3, 4 as you breathe out.
- Roll some breaths from belly to chest like a wave. Breathe half of the inhalation into your abdomen, allowing your belly to rise. Pause. Then roll the rest of your in-breath into your mid-chest, feeling your ribcage expand out to the sides. Exhale slowly. Repeat five times.
- Constrict your throat slightly so the air makes a soft wave-like sound. Spend a few minutes just listening.

All of the above double as useful anti-insomnia techniques, ensuring you get a quality, deep sleep the night before a competition, and are not still awake at 2 a.m. running through kit lists or wondering when the alarm will go off. For home-based relaxation and meditation techniques turn to Chapter 11.

BALANCE TRAINING

‘ *Improving balance and proprioception is something, along with core strengthening, that can boost performance and help an athlete stay injury free. I often recommend yoga when treating injured runners because it addresses both these areas, and advise practising yoga and balances daily as a preventative measure.* ’

Dr Brian Fullem, podiatrist

Yoga balances could have been designed specifically for runners; they strengthen your feet and ankles to better absorb the impact of running, improve proprioception and hone concentration skills (if your mind wavers, the body wobbles and you fall).

Balancing postures benefit all runners, but particularly trail specialists who need to rapidly sense the position of their limbs in space on rocky or uneven terrain. Runners considering going barefoot will also need to mobilise and strengthen their feet before venturing outside without trainers.

This chapter contains a variety of balances from the static tree, a posture that demands absolute focus, to dynamic running-specific sequences that will test agility, power and precision.

THE BENEFITS OF BALANCES

1 Strengthens your feet and ankles

Remove your shoes and socks, stand in front of a mirror and balance on one foot. Observe how the fine muscles of your feet rapidly contract and release to stabilise your entire body. Watching your foot and ankle working, it's clear to see how even a simple balance can reinforce your lower limbs to cope with the rigours of running.

Unless you are a seasoned barefoot runner your feet are cushioned inside shoes – be it leather shoes or trainers – for the vast majority of the day. Unchallenged, the muscles of your feet and ankles become weak and vulnerable to acute injuries, such as twisted ankles, especially if you are running on rough, bumpy ground, or at night-time, when visibility is poor.

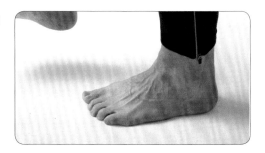

Weakened foot arches also put pressure on the plantar fascia – the superficial layer of connective tissue running from toes to heel. This can result in common overuse injuries such as plantar fasciitis or inflammation of the connective tissue on the sole of the foot.

In fact the feet are engineered to excel at traversing uneven terrain. They comprise four layers of musculature and 28 bones designed to soak up the forces generated by walking and running.

Yoga, generally, is ideal for reawakening this natural strength due to the fact that classes are always done barefoot. However, balances will greatly accelerate this strengthening process.

Many have the added benefit to not just reinforcing your feet and ankles but your entire leg, sometimes honing in on your glutes, hip flexors or quads, while others will combine balancing and stretching.

2 Improves balance and proprioception

Our physiological sense of balance comprises a number of different systems – the vestibular (inner ear), visual (eyes) and sense of proprioception (body's awareness of the orientation of its limbs in space). All these systems combine to allow us to walk or run without keeling over or constantly monitoring our foot placement.

A superior sense of balance also aids agility in trail or hill running. For example, the proprioceptors, or sensory receptors located within muscles and tendons, respond to changes in body or limb position, allowing the runner to traverse with accuracy and precision.

The proprioceptors might inform the muscles to fire to prevent an ankle rolling over causing a potential sprain. 'Balance and proprioception play an extremely important role in the normal function of the body's tendons and muscles', explains podiatrist, Dr Brian Fullem.

Dr Fullem offers running clients a simple 'proprioception function test' – standing on one leg with the eyes closed. If you immediately thrust the hands out or are forced to put the foot down, work on training the proprioceptors by repeating the exercise. First do it wearing trainers with the eyes open until you can hold for a minute. Then try it barefoot with the eyes open, and finally go barefoot, reverting back to closing the eyes.

Trail running and balance

The three main benefits of balances – bolstering your feet and ankles to withstand impact, improving your sense of balance and honing concentration skills – are particularly beneficial for hill or trail runners. Their bodies must alter their centre of gravity continually to allow the legs to keep moving at a good pace, whatever the terrain. This ability to move gracefully wasting minimum energy, knowing the exact position of that right foot and where it will land next, can be improved by practising both the static and dynamic balancing sequences in this chapter, particularly the running-specific techniques.

HOW TO BALANCE

Step 1:
Broaden your base

Nothing can be built on a shaky foundation. The first step, therefore, is to spend a moment broadening your base – your feet. Stand with your feet hip-distance apart. Lift and spread your toes, then lay them down, aiming to glimpse some yoga mat, or floor, between each toe. Lift the arches of your feet. Now place equal weight on the four 'corners' of your feet – your big toe, little toe, inner heel and outer heel.

Step 2:
Stand tall

Balancing requires good overall posture, as well as stability in your legs and core, so begin every balance in mountain pose (see page 25). Focus first on your feet, then let your attention move up your legs and spine, right to the top of your head. Lengthen from feet to crown. Tuck your pelvis under and lightly engage your abdomen.

Step 3:
Slow the breathing

Slow, deep, abdominal breathing focuses the mind and steadies your body in balances. Rapid panting or upper chest breathing will make you top heavy and more likely to topple. Switch to nasal breathing and start to slow your respiration. Relax your abdomen and breathe more into your belly. Make the exhalation slightly longer than the inhalation. Take a moment to listen to the soothing sound of your breath – don't be rushed.

Step 4:
Find a 'gaze point'

Choose a point on a wall directly ahead or on the floor and 'fix' your gaze to this point. In yoga this gazing technique is called *drishti*. Often this refers to staring at one spot, but holding your gaze has the wider purpose of forging a meditative state. Gazing steadily outwards while holding postures settles your mind (looking out to draw your attention inwards). In purely physiological terms, when your eyes focus on a steady object, your inner ear can orient your head vertically, horizontally and spatially, which helps stabilise your body.

Step 5:
Hold the pose

Once your body is steadied through deep breathing and gazing at a fixed point, hold the pose for five to ten breaths. If you are new to balancing and very wobbly take heart – balancing improves with practice, just like any skill. Try practicing with a wall close behind to lean back on if necessary and stand on a hard surface (wooden or tiled floor) rather than soft carpet. Feeling steady? Hold for longer, try to grip with your toes less and experiment with closing your eyes for a few seconds.

Everyday balances

Balance – like all other skills – improves with practice. The trick is to incorporate it into everyday life. While cleaning your teeth shift your weight onto one foot and balance like a stork, switching sides halfway through. If the doorbell rings, walk to answer it on the balls or heels of your feet. Waiting in a queue at the bank? Rise slowly onto your toes and lower down three or four times. Not only are you honing balance, but also strengthening your lower limbs and guarding against shin splints and Achilles tendonitis.

FOOT FOUNDATION SEQUENCE

This series of basic balances created by Yoga Sports Science® can be used to assess both the sense of balance, and strength of the feet and ankles. It would suit all runners and especially those venturing into barefoot running. The idea is to rise directly upwards onto the balls of your feet without swaying forwards or backwards or rocking onto the inner or outer edges of your feet.

1 **Mountain pose:** Stand in mountain pose with your feet hip-distance apart. Draw your shoulders back and down. Lift and spread your toes. Press the 'four corners' of your feet – big toes, little toes, inner heel and outer heel – into the floor. Stand tall.

2 **Circling balance:** Close your eyes and visualise a circle above your head like a large angel's halo. Now move your whole body around this circle feeling your weight shifting around the soles of your feet. Return to mountain pose allowing your body to settle and find its natural plumb line.

3 **Rising and lowering:** Slowly rise onto the balls of your feet as if you were being pulled, like a puppet, directly upwards. Try not to lean forwards or rock back and keep your feet and ankles still. Lower gradually down and repeat four times working with your breath – inhaling up and exhaling down.

4 Sweep the arms: Once happy with step 3, include your arms by sweeping both arms to the ceiling as you rise onto your toes. Try not to let your back buckle as you raise your arms. Return your arms as you lower down. Repeat four times.

5 Toe walking: Rise onto your toes and walk slowly around the outer edge of the mat, returning to the front.

6 Heel walking: Shift your weight onto your heels and lift your toes off the floor. Walk slowly around the outer edge of the mat.

Barefoot running and yoga

Shoes are left at the door in a yoga class, which is why it is a good discipline for those wanting to prep their feet for barefoot running. The expert advice is to allow a few months just walking around barefoot before attempting to run. This is because our feet are usually cushioned inside shoes and therefore unprepared for the impact of running barefoot. In yoga all the standing postures begin from the feet up and time is taken to improve the flexibility, strength and responsiveness of the feet. A regular yoga practice, with its barefoot balances, standing postures and general foot awareness, is an ideal way to prepare the feet to go shoe-less. See Chapter 5 for more foot techniques suited both to barefoot and shod runners.

BALANCING POSTURES

Hold each static pose for five to ten breaths.

The stork

The stork is a simple balance and, therefore, an ideal one to practise applying the 'how to balance' principles outlined on page 54. The action of drawing your leg into your abdomen also gently stretches your hamstrings and releases lower back tension making it a perfect post-run balance.

Stand in mountain pose. Widen your base by spreading your toes. Shift your weight onto your left foot. Slowly hug your right leg in towards your abdomen but remain standing tall lifting from the crown of your head.

Modify: Perform with your back very close to, or against, the wall.
Advance: Slowly rotate the foot of your hugged-in leg.

Tree balance

This iconic yoga posture is a good all-rounder for runners. It works the feet and ankles of your standing leg and provides a hip and adductor stretch for your bent leg. Taking your arms wide improves posture by easing back your shoulders and opening your chest.

Stand in mountain pose. Spread your toes and shift your weight onto your right foot. Contract the muscles of your standing leg – this is your firm tree trunk. Turn your left leg out and place the sole of your left foot on the inside of your right thigh or lower onto your ankle. Raise your arms to shoulder-height and spread them wide. Turn your palms up and draw your arms slightly back to open your chest.

Modify:

1 Practise with your back resting against the wall.
2 Start low, with your foot resting against your ankle.

Advance:

1 Bring your palms together to create a feeling of calm.
2 Sweep both arms up overhead and bring your palms together.
3 To further challenge your sense of balance close your eyes.

Swaying tree

To really test the stability of your tree, make it sway in the wind.

Drop your right hand down and rest it lightly on your right thigh. Breathe in. As you exhale, side bend over to the right and sweep your left arm over. Hold for two or three breaths and return to the centre. Repeat on the other side.

Dancer's pose

Dancer's pose is a must-have for runners. It both strengthens the lower limb of your standing leg and stretches the quad and hip flexor of your bent leg.

Stand in mountain pose. Shift your weight onto your right foot and bend your left leg. Reach behind with your left hand and hold onto the front of your foot. Tuck your pelvis under to minimise the lower back arch and line up your knees. Sweep your right arm up and tuck your first finger under the thumb to make a circle or keep the palm open as shown. As you breathe out, first push your foot into your hand to draw back your leg like a bow. Either remain here or hinge forwards from your hips keeping your back straight.

Modify:

1 Perform facing a wall so you can rest your fingertips on its surface.
2 Loop a strap around your foot if tight quads prevent you grasping it.

Advance:

1 Tip further forwards and raise your back leg higher.
2 Drop the circle you have made with your hands in line with your vision and gaze through it.

Warrior 3

Warrior 3 strengthens the hamstrings and glutes. Performed with your arms stretched out in front it also reinforces your back muscles making it a great all-round balance to improve running power and posture.

Stand in mountain pose with your hands on your hips. Raise your left leg up as you tip forwards into a right-angle position. Point your left toes down and aim to line up your leg with your spine. Level your hips. Slowly sweep both arms out in front and parallel so your palms face. Gaze down at the floor.

Modify:

1 Rest the sole of your back foot against the wall.
2 Rest your fingertips against a wall.
3 Take your arms out sideways like a tightrope walker.
4 Place your hands on your hips.

Half-moon balance

Half-moon pose doubles up as a lateral and core strengthener.

Stand in the middle of your mat and place your feet wide apart. Turn your right foot out and left foot 45° inwards. If using a block, place it in the top right hand corner of the mat. Bend your front leg and lower your right fingertips or palm to the floor (or block). Take your top hand to your waist. Slowly raise your back leg up. Now rotate your torso outwards as if you wanted to turn your abdomen to the ceiling. Draw your top shoulder back. To advance, extend your top arm up and spread your fingers.

Modify:

1 Practise against a wall leaning the back of your body into its surface for support.
2 Place two to three yoga blocks, or books, under your front hand to raise the floor level.

Advance:

1 Perform without the block.
2 Slide your lower hand up to knee height.

Half-moon quad stretch

This challenging variation of half-moon requires not just solid balancing skills but also supple hip flexors and quads. If mastered, however, it will lengthen your thigh and anterior hip muscles while strengthening your standing leg and drawing back your top shoulder – multi-tasking as only yoga poses can.

Modify:

1 Hook a strap or tie around your foot.
2 Place two to three yoga blocks, or books, under your front hand to raise the floor level.

Leg strength balance

This balance is a pure strengthening pose, challenging both legs and the hip flexors of your standing leg – the muscles at the top of your thigh that lift your leg as you run. Avoid it if your hip flexors are tight, or sore from running and follow with dancer's pose to stretch out your muscles.

Stand in mountain pose and place your hands on your hips. Shift your weight on to your right leg and lift your left leg up, keeping it straight. Point your toes to the ceiling. Stay for five to ten breaths lifting your leg a little on each inhalation.

Advance:

Lift your leg higher – aiming to create a right angle position.

RUNNING-SPECIFIC BALANCE

Stride sequences

The following sequences pair balance with your running leg swing motion. The first stage gets your body accustomed to a simple leg swinging action. The second strengthening phase links two yoga postures: leg strength balance and warrior 3. The third sequence is more running-specific and includes a rise into the ball of your foot to further challenge the balance.

Aim for slow, fluid movements. Let your arms swing in opposition to your leg just as if you were running. Begin by swinging your left leg. Repeat each stage four times.

1 BASIC LEG SWING

Begin with a simple leg swinging motion. Spread the toes of your standing leg to aid with balance. Let your breath flow freely.

2 LEG STRENGTH BALANCE TO WARRIOR 3

Lift your swinging leg higher up, pointing your toes to the ceiling. Draw it back and sweep it slowly behind you tipping your upper body forwards. Aim to make a 90° shape with your legs. Inhale to swing up, and exhale to swing back.

3 STRIDE BALANCE

Slightly bend both legs and arms to create a more realistic running movement. Lift your swinging leg up and rise on to the ball of your standing leg for an extra challenge. As you exhale lower back to your heel and draw your swinging leg back. Lean forwards to exaggerate the movement.

Lunge sequence

Develop agility, power and precision with this dynamic sequence. These Yoga Sports Science® techniques are particularly useful for trail runners who need a superior sense of proprioception to place their feet quickly and accurately.

Lunges are also fantastic for working your quads and glutes in a running-specific way. Finally, side lunges shift runners out of their forwards-only plane of motion creating balanced leg strength.

- **Step to exactly the same point each time.** If using a yoga mat step to the top line of the mat. Or place a marker just above the toes of your stepping up foot.
- **Ensure the knee doesn't come forwards of the ankle** to avoid putting pressure on your joint.
- **Move slowly, with control** to maintain precision.
- **Work with your breath:** Synchronise the movement and breathing by inhaling in mountain, exhaling to lunge and inhaling back to mountain.
- **Step lightly:** Engage the core to create a soft, quiet step up and back.
- **Repeat four times, alternating legs.**

1 STEP-UP LUNGES

Stand in mountain pose at the rear of your mat with your hands on your hips. As you exhale step your right foot up into a lunge, roll on to the ball of your back foot. Inhale and push off from your foot to step back to mountain. For a further challenge repeat the technique with your eyes closed.

2 STEP-UP TWISTS

Repeat step 1 but this time fold your arms and as you step lift the right foot up and slowly rotate your torso to the left. Inhale and return to standing. Step up with your left leg and twist to the right.

3 STEP-BACK LUNGES

Stand in mountain pose with your hands on your hips. This time, as you exhale, step your right foot back to the block. Inhale and push off from your back foot to return to mountain. Step your left leg back.

4 SIDE LUNGES

Stand in mountain pose with your hands on your hips. Turn 90° to the right. On an exhale step your right foot wide and bend your knees into a lunge, ensuring your knee doesn't come forwards of your toes. Turn your toes slightly outwards. Inhale, push off your foot and return to standing. Repeat three times, then rotate 180° and repeat your side lunges stepping your left leg wide.

Walking lunge warm-up

For a dynamic warm-up that will improve balance, stretch your calves, glutes and hip flexors and forge running power try this plyometric sequence.

Stand tall. Perform stork by hugging your right leg into your abdomen and lengthen your spine.

On an exhale step your right foot forwards and lower into a lunge.

Inhale and lift your left leg and hug it into your abdomen.

Exhale and lower forwards a lunge.

Continue five times on each side, synching movement and breath.

To advance the technique rise onto the ball of the foot while in stork.

BALANCED STRETCH SEQUENCE

This sequence will test your sense of balance and stretch many classic running tight spots, including your hamstrings, adductors, quads and glutes. Practise it with your back against the wall to begin with, if you are new to balancing, and attempt it free standing when you feel ready to do so. Flexible runners can hold onto the big toe with the first two fingers rather than use a strap but either way, ensure your hamstrings are warmed up first.

You will need a cotton yoga strap, resistance band, old tie or dressing gown belt. Hold each section of the sequence for five to ten breaths.

1 STANDING HAMSTRING STRETCH

Balance on your left foot and loop the strap around the sole of your right foot. Flex your foot. As you inhale slowly raise your leg up until you feel the hamstrings stretching. Adjust the strap if it is slack. Maintain straight arms but stand tall, lifting from the crown of your head.

2 STANDING ADDUCTOR STRETCH

Sweep your leg slowly out to the right holding both parts of the strap in your right hand. Keep your foot flexed. Extend your left arm out to make a diagonal line from left fingertips to right heel. To advance rotate your head to look towards the left hand.

3 GLUTE/ILIOTIBIAL BAND STRETCH

Return your leg to the position in step 1. Grasp both parts of the strap with your left hand. Draw your leg across your body and extend your right arm out for balance making a diagonal line from right fingertips to left heel. To advance, rotate your head to look to your right hand.

4 QUAD STRETCH

Return your leg to the position in step 1. Bend it, lower your foot and move it back into a quad stretch. Take your right hand back and hold onto your foot. Tuck the sacrum in and draw your foot back to deepen the stretch. Ease your shoulders back to open your chest and stand tall. Stay for five breaths.

LOWER LEG STRETCHES

❝ During the course of an average mile run, your foot will strike the ground 1,000 times. The force of impact on each foot is about three to four times your weight. It's not surprising, then, to hear runners complain of bad backs and knees, tight hamstrings, and sore feet. ❞

Baron Baptise and Kathleen Finn Mendola,
www.yogajournal.com

Supple, strong and responsive feet are fundamental in yoga, partly due to the belief that no standing posture can be built on weak foundations. This concept of strong foot foundations transfers well to running, where the lower limbs are required to soak up such forces on every stride.

An inability to absorb the impact of running can create numerous issues further up the body, especially for barefoot runners who lack the protection of cushioned trainers. This chapter offers a range of yoga techniques and stretches for our interface between the ground and the body: the feet, ankles, shins and calves.

THE FEET

The feet can be a vulnerable part of a runner's anatomy. Plantar fasciitis, or inflammation of the connective tissue on the sole of the foot, is especially common among road runners (see box on page 77). Yet most runners rarely stretch their feet. Regular stretching and strength work, will create strong but pliable feet better able to cope with the rigours of running and reduce the chances of injury. The improved responsiveness aids balance and agility required for trails and primes your feet for barefoot running. For complementary strengthening exercises, turn to the previous chapter's balances.

Fanning the toes

Stand in mountain pose with your feet hip-distance apart. Lift your toes off the floor. Hold for a few seconds with your toes splayed wide, then lay them down again. Aim to glimpse a small section of floor or yoga mat between each toe. This is a simple way to stretch your feet and provides a wide, stable base for balancing.

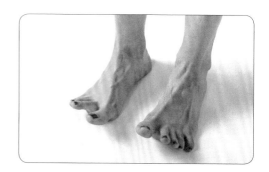

Mexican toe wave

It might be a while before your feet are ready to do a full Mexican wave, but it's an interesting experiment in foot muscle coordination to try! Begin by breaking the exercise down into sections. First lift your big toes and lower. Next keep your big toes grounded and raise the rest of your toes. Repeat the exercise little and often. Graduate to peeling all your toes off one by one, from large to small.

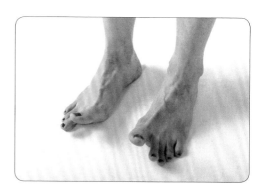

Ankle rotations

Simply rotate your foot in slow circles either standing and balancing on one leg, or lying on your back with your foot elevated. Concentrate on creating smooth circles and notice any areas of resistance.

Picking up marbles

The action of picking up marbles with your feet pumps blood into the sole of your foot and increases flexibility. If marbles are too small then begin with a larger object, such as a golf ball or grab dirty socks off the floor with your feet and drop them into the laundry bin, challenging your sense of balance. The trick is to make these exercises part of everyday life so pick pens up off the floor or take the bath plug out with your toes.

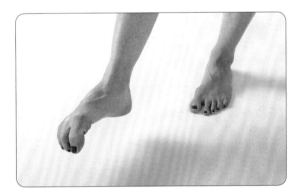

Toe writing

Toe writing is a fun way to keep the muscles of your feet and ankles supple. It can be done sitting or standing to challenge your sense of balance. Elevate one foot and point your toes. Now write your full name by tracing the letters in the air.

Cobbler's pose massage

Yoga's cobbler's pose (page 96) is a great posture to access your feet while simultaneously stretching your hips and adductors. Bend your legs and draw the soles of your feet together.

Now try the following:

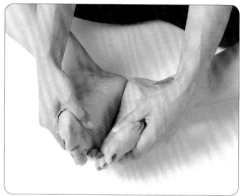

1 **Open book:** Hold the sides of your feet and ease them open, as if opening the pages of a book.

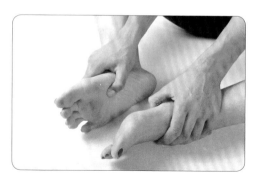

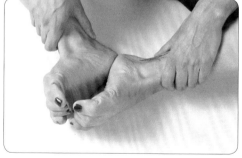

2 **Sole massage:** Using your thumb, slowly massage the sole of your foot by pressing and releasing. Work your way from the heel to the ball of each foot and back down again.

3 **Toe scrunching:** Move your toes in the opposite direction by curling them tightly. Hold for a few seconds and then release.

4 **Toe pull backs:** Lightly grip your toes and ease them back. Hold for a few seconds, then release.

Plantar fasciitis stretch

This stretch may make you grimace, especially after eight miles pounding the pavements. The combination of curling your toes up and stretching the soles of your feet in steps 1–3 can feel intense, so ease in gently or perform the cobbler's pose massage first.

1 Get down on all fours and turn your toes under so you are on the balls of your feet. Glance back between your knees to ensure that your toes are spread evenly. If this is enough, remain here breathing steadily.

2 Slowly begin to move backwards, inching towards a kneeling position. You may need to stop halfway with your fingertips resting on the floor. If comfortable, sit all the way back on your heels with a straight back.

Plantar fasciitis

'Walking on glass' is how runners suffering with severe plantar fasciitis describe the pain, especially when first stepping out of bed in the morning. This discomfort is caused by the inflammation of the plantar fascia – a layer of connective tissue that connects the toes to the heel and absorbs the shock of running and walking. Causes include the repetitive motion of long-distance running, especially road running, but also tight calves and Achilles tendons. Help prevent plantar fasciitis with regular stretching and mobility exercises for the soles of the feet, but don't forget to lengthen the Achilles and calves. Massaging the plantar fascia by lifting the big toe and massaging with the thumb can also help, as can rolling a golf ball underfoot. See a physiotherapist at the first hint of discomfort for advice on treatment.

3 Ease slowly back to all fours, lift each foot and make slow rotations.

THE CALVES

Another running shock absorber, the calves and Achilles tendon are prone to injury, especially among sprinters and hill runners but also long-distance athletes. Thankfully, there are 101 ways to stretch tight calf muscles. Many yoga postures will also lengthen tight calves, especially pyramid and downward facing dog, and come with numerous other benefits (particularly lengthening your hamstrings) if you want more of a 'whole-body' approach.

The squat test

How do you know if your calf muscles are tight? Performing a squat test will give a good indication of flexibility levels in this area. Stand with your feet shoulder-width apart and toes slightly turned out. Slowly lower down into a squat, ensuring that your knee tracks over your second toe. Note the angle of your legs when your heels peel off the floor. Less than a 90° bend in your knee indicates tight calves. Lowering all the way to the floor with your heels still firmly grounded indicates good calf flexibility, but even the most supple runner would benefit from regular stretching.

Squat, don't bend

Dropped something? It's instinctive to hinge at your waist or lower back to pick it up. The same folding stance is often used to communicate with dogs or toddlers, or to stack groceries in a low cupboard. Providing your knees are healthy, try squatting instead. This stance places no pressure on your lower back and actually releases lower back tension. Squatting also strengthens and lengthens your calves, improves range of motion in your hips and gives your quads and glutes a good workout on the way down and up.

Squat variations
Experiment with the following variations to find a squat to suit.

Wall squat: If tight calves cause you to tip backwards in a squat practise with your back leaning against the wall. Begin standing and slowly lower down, maintaining back contact with the surface.

Doorknob squat: For a bonus stretch in your shoulders and upper back, hold onto a doorknob and lower down into the squat so that your arms are straight. Relax your head.

Swaying squat: Bring your fingertips to the floor for balance and sway from side to side working a little deeper into your hips.

Prayer squat: To increase the intensity of the squat (and providing your heels are close to, or on, the floor for balance) bring your palms together in a prayer position so your elbows are inside your knees. Drop your forearms down so they form a straight line.

Feet together squat: Lower down with your feet together. The heels will probably rise up but just drop your fingertips to the floor and breathe slowly. This is a good calf preparation for the more intense downward facing dog.

Rolled mat stretch

Roll up your mat, beginning at the top and continuing until roughly halfway down. Now place the balls of your feet on the roll so your feet are dorsiflexed (toes towards shins). This may be sufficient to feel the muscles of the back of your lower leg lengthening. To move deeper into the stretch come into a slow forward-bend by bending your knees and folding forwards. Either come halfway down or rest your fingertips on the floor.

Step/block stretch

A similar stretch can be performed on one or two foam yoga blocks, thick hardback books or on the edge of the stairs. Lie the block on the floor, stand on the edge of it and lower one heel down. If practising on a step try dropping both heels. To further stretch and strengthen your calves and ankles (and improve balance) begin on the balls of your feet and lower down past the step. Now rise all the way back up.

Windscreen wiping

To stretch your calves in a runner's lunge position, shift your body weight back towards your heel and roll front foot back onto your heel so your toes point upwards. Now 'windscreen wipe' your foot by swaying it slowly from side to side. Pause in any section of the movement, drop your fingertips to the floor and take a few breaths if you find a tight spot. This stretch is part of the post-run lunge sequence featured at the end of the next chapter (see page 98).

Sprint stretch

Step your left foot back and bend your right leg. Ensure both feet are facing forwards. Drop your fingertips to the floor. Slowly draw your back heel down towards the floor.

Pyramid

Pyramid is a staple yoga pose for runners. It lengthens tight hamstrings and calves and will decompress your spine if performed with your hands resting on a wall or chair. Ensure your feet always face front and are hip-distance apart.

HALF PYRAMID

Half pyramid stretches your calf and hamstring while strengthening your back. Begin with your feet hip-width and step your right foot forward. Keep the toes of both feet facing front. Sweep your arms behind your back and hold onto your elbows. On an exhalation, forward-bend to a 90° position. Take five slow breaths, or more if well balanced. Maintain a long, straight spine. To exit engage your abdomen, bend your front knee and rise up.

FULL PYRAMID

Repeat half pyramid but release your fingertips all the way down to the floor, placing them either side of your feet. If they don't reach the floor, bend your front leg more or place a block – or stack of books – under each hand. Release your head.

'Walking dog' – a pre-run warm-up

Downwards facing dog is another fantastic pose for runners as it lengthens your hamstrings and calves and builds upper body strength. The only problem with dog for runners is that tight hamstrings and calves (combined with a stiff back and hips) can cause your back to round, placing extra weight on your hands and shoulders. 'Walking dog' eases this pressure a little by bending one leg and is an excellent way to dynamically warm up your calves pre-run.

Begin on all fours. Spread your fingers and slowly lift your hips towards the ceiling. Keep your legs bent and draw your hips to the back of the room to lengthen your back as much as possible. Now keeping your breathing slow bend one leg and draw your opposite heel to the floor. Continue, speeding up and moving from side to side.

Achilles tendonitis

The Achilles tendon connects the two main calf muscles to the back of your heel. If you run a lot harder or further than usual, or have tight or weak calves, you are at risk of irritating or inflaming the tendon. If there is any pain see a physiotherapist who might recommend strengthening and stretching techniques. Regular and gentle stretching, in the meantime, is a good preventative measure.

Static dog

Provided there is sufficient flexibility in the hamstrings to shift the weight onto the back of the body so that it doesn't feel like a plank, dog is a very effective calf stretch. In static dog both heels are drawn to the floor and held there for 30-60 seconds. Begin in all fours. Spread your fingers and slowly lift the hips towards the ceiling.

Modify: Bend the knees or perform walking dog.
Advance: To deepen the calf stretch place two blocks under each hand to raise the upper body.

THE SHINS

The shin muscles work with your toe extensors to lift your foot as you run making them susceptible to injury if they are not both strong and supple enough to handle the repetitive nature of running.

Standing shin stretch

The most accessible and simple way to stretch your shins is to step your foot behind you and place the front of your foot on the floor, as if you were dragging a limp leg behind you. Now press into the floor until you feel a stretch in the foot and shin.

Kneeling shin/ankle stretch

This stretch places pressure on your ankles and knee so opt for the standing version if deep flexion is uncomfortable. Begin in a kneeling position with your hands resting either side of your feet. Now lean back and lift your knees off the ground so you roll onto the front of your feet.

Shin splints

The term 'shin splints' refers to an inflammation of your shin muscles as they expand and swell in training and are then compressed against the bone. This pressure can cut off blood supply, leading to pain. Causes range from short, tight or weak shin muscles, running on hard surfaces, and a lack of adequate cushioning in running shoes. Many of the stretches in this chapter, both for your shins and Achilles tendons, serve as good preventative measures. Strengthening the area may also help; see the 'heel walking' exercise in Chapter 4 (page 57). But seek advice from a physiotherapist first if you are already suffering with shin splints.

LOWER LIMB SEQUENCE

Link some of the previous techniques into a sequence to stretch the plantar fascia, shins and calves and strengthen your feet and ankles. This routine requires the ability both to kneel and spread your toes in order to comfortably stretch and distribute body weight through your feet. Deep foot stretching can trigger cramp if done immediately after a long run so wait an hour or practise this sequence between runs.

Take four breaths in each step.

1 **All fours sole stretch:** Come onto all fours and turn your toes under. Glance back between your knees to ensure that your toes are spread evenly. If this is enough, remain here.

2 **Kneeling sole stretch:** Slowly lower your hips back towards your heels. Either keep your fingers on the floor or lift your torso up into a kneeling position, resting your palms on your thighs.

3 **Kneeling balance:** Lift your knees off the floor and bring your palms together to perform a balance. Gaze ahead.

4 **Low squat:** Lower your heels to the floor to stretch your calves. Drop your fingertips to the floor.

5 All fours: Return to all fours, but rest the front of your feet on the floor.

6 Basic kneeling: Lower into a kneeling position, placing your hands on your thighs.

7 Kneeling shin stretch: Place your hands either side of your feet and raise your knees off the floor.

8 Foot drumming: Return to all fours and 'drum' your feet by gently tapping the front of your feet on the floor.

06

UPPER LEG STRETCHES

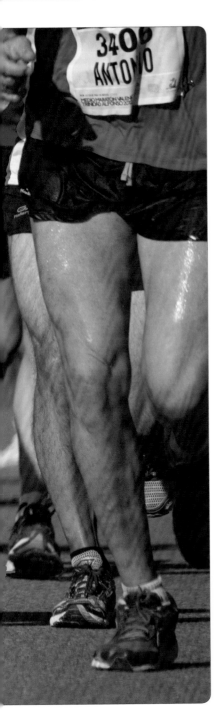

' Before I took up yoga I was struggling on and off with various injuries, mainly stemming from tight hips and surrounding muscles. After taking up a weekly post-run yoga session I saw improvements almost immediately, have been injury-free and am running PBs every race. '

**Daniel Everall, 10K, half-marathon
and marathon runner, Surrey, UK**

By unlocking tight hips, glutes, quads and hamstrings through targeted stretches, runners can create a longer and more fluid stride. Regularly lengthening these running tight spots also reduces the chances of suffering common overuse running injuries such as iliotibial band syndrome and piriformis syndrome.

The stretches in this chapter are divided into anatomical sections for easy reference, although many yoga postures – such as pigeon – defy this classification as they target several muscle groups simultaneously. Cherry-pick one or two from each anatomical section to target a specific area, or try an 'all-in-one' post-run leg sequence such as post run lunge or post run strap to restore overall leg muscle balance.

THE HAMSTRINGS

It's rare to meet a runner who doesn't complain of tight hamstrings, but there are many ways to maintain the elasticity of semimembranosus, semitendinosus and biceps femoris. Whether standing, sitting or lying just remember to hold for a good 30–60 seconds which equates to five to ten slow breaths. A quick 5-second tug on your hamstrings is of little benefit. Have patience. Rather than seeing hamstring stretching as a chore think of it as mini relaxation: sit, or lie back, close your eyes and tune into your breathing.

How to stretch tight hamstrings

1 **Bend your knees:** If performing a forward-bending hamstring stretch, bend your knees to take the strain off your lower back.

2 **Sit on a block:** Perch on the edge of a block or cushion in the seated stretches. This tips your pelvis into an anterior tilt which, again, takes the pressure off your lower back.

3 **Use a strap:** In seated and lying hamstring stretches go for comfort, and a more targeted hamstring stretch, by looping a yoga strap, old tie or dressing gown belt around the sole of your foot.

4 **Don't round your back:** In seated forward-bends imagine folding chest to knee, not nose to knee. Rounding and pushing down in the hope of inching your nose closer just strains the lumber region.

5 **Don't bounce:** In response to every bounce your hamstrings will contract tighter. Instead be still and breathe slowly to facilitate a slow, gradual release.

6 **Have patience:** It takes at least 30 seconds for your hamstrings to release. Use this time to close your eyes, tune into your breath and recharge mental and physical batteries.

7 **Don't strain:** It is possible to overstretch hamstrings so never force it. Find the 'edge' of the stretch and only inch further when the muscles are ready. Sweating or shaking are signs of too much too soon.

8 **Stretch post-run:** As with all deep, static stretching, save it until after the run. Pre-run opt for a dynamic hamstring stretching movement such as 'toy soldier' straight leg marching.

Left: *How to stretch the hamstrings*
Above: *How not to stretch the hamstrings*

Standing hamstring stretches

90° HAMSTRING STRETCH

To stretch tight hamstrings without straining your back try this half-forward-bend. Stand with your feet hip-distance, toes facing front. Inhale, and on an exhalation slide your hands down your thighs to rest just above your knees. Tilt your pelvis under to minimise the lumbar curve. Look downwards. Exit safely (see box below).

FULL FORWARD-BEND

To stretch deeper repeat the 90° stretch, but slide your hands down until your fingertips touch the floor either side of your feet. Bend your knees as much as you need to (or raise the floor level by resting your fingertips on some blocks or books). Exit safely (see box below).

Exiting forward-bends

Use the following procedure to exit safely from forward-bends without loading the lumbar spine.

1 Bend your knees and rise up halfway to the 90° stretch.

2 Pause. Engage your abdomen. Take your hands to your hips.

3 Bend your knees, and on an inhalation, hinge all the way to standing with a flat back, like a weightlifter.

HAMSTRING AND UPPER BACK RELEASE

Dissolve upper back, neck and shoulder tension by performing a forward-bend, then folding your arms. Let the full weight of your arms hang down. Swing from side to side like a pendulum. For a bonus neck stretch interlace your hands behind your neck and relax your arms. Exit safely (see box on previous page).

Hamstring strengthening

Hamstrings need to be both pliable and strong to avoid injury. Bridge pose – especially hamstring bridge – is a simple way to strengthen this area without the need for gym equipment. Other good postures include warrior 2 and side angle pose as both combine strengthening with lengthening to create long, lean muscles. See Chapter 7 and Chapter 8 for details of these postures.

Floor hamstring stretches

SEATED HAMSTRING STRETCH

Sit on the edge of a block or cushion and loop a strap around the soles of your feet. Straighten your legs, or create a small bend in your knees. Sit tall and inhale. As you breathe out, inch your hands down the strap until you feel your back become round and your hamstrings pull. Stop. Relax your head, close your eyes and hold, subtly moving your chest – not your nose – towards your knees. Lower back discomfort? Rise up higher.

SEATED HAMSTRING/ HIP STRETCH

Remain in the same position, but bend your left leg and take the sole of your left foot to the inside of your right thigh. Place a cushion or block under your knee if it is hovering off the floor. Sit tall and inhale. As you breathe out walk your hands down the strap until you feel your back become round and your hamstrings pull. Relax your head, close your eyes and breathe slowly encouraging your chest gradually closer to your knee. Rise up.

STRAP HAMSTRING STRETCH

A simple and relaxing way to stretch your hamstrings is to lie on your back, loop a strap around the sole of your right foot and straighten your leg as much as your hamstrings allow. Bend your left leg and place your foot on the floor or – for a more advanced version – extend it along the floor with your left toes pointing upwards and press the back of your knee into the floor. Walk your hands up the strap until your arms straighten.

THE QUADS

Stretching the four 'quads' at the front of your thigh will increase blood flow, helping to repair micro tears, and restore your muscles to their resting length. This is especially important after speed work, sprinting or hill runs.

However, compared with a simple hamstring stretch, lengthening your quads can feel awkward, partly because they pass through your knee joint. That's fine if your joint is supple and injury-free, but it can exacerbate any existing problems. The golden rule is if there's any discomfort, exit your stretch and substitute one with less knee impact.

The quad section of this chapter contains a range of stretches that should be accessible to all runners. As with hamstring stretching, a little patience reaps rewards, so maintain for at least 30 seconds.

BASIC QUAD STRETCH

Stand with your feet hip-distance apart, facing a wall ready to rest your fingertips on the surface for balance. Bend your left leg and reach back for your foot with your left hand. If your foot is beyond your grasp, loop the strap around it. Level your knees and tuck your pelvis under. To advance this stretch try dancer's pose in Chapter 4 (page 60).

SHOULDER/QUAD STRETCH

Set up the stretch as before but move a little further away from the wall. Bend your right leg and reach back for your foot with your right hand, using the strap if necessary. Walk your left fingertips up the wall and lean into the surface until you feel your shoulder and upper arm stretch. Keep your pelvis tucked under. Walk your fingertips back down to rise up.

LYING QUAD STRETCH

Stretching while lying on your side is often the most comfortable position for those with tight quads or stiff knees. Have the strap nearby and lie on one side. Bend your top leg and hold your foot, or loop the strap around it. Extend your lower arm and rest your head on it.

The kneeling series

The series of postures below are based on yoga's basic kneeling position (virasana). Kneeling provides a gentle quad stretch and stretches the front of your feet and ankles – a good combination for runners. However, kneeling brings your legs into deep flexion placing pressure on your knee joint and ligaments so those with knee injuries, or stiff ankles, may find it uncomfortable or impossible. If this is you, just practise step 1 with plenty of padding or opt for standing quad stretches. As the series proceeds the postures become stronger, so continue to monitor your knees and your lower back.

You will need some foam yoga blocks or cushions.

1 **Kneeling:** Sit in a kneeling position with your heels together. To lessen the knee flexion place one or more cushions between your buttocks and heels. Or separate your heels and lay two to three yoga blocks horizontally between your lower legs. Rest your palms on your thighs and sit tall. Gaze ahead or close your eyes.

2 **Half kneeling quad stretch:** From kneeling release your right foot out and place it on the floor with your leg still bent. Take your hands behind you, fingers pointing backwards. Lift your hips off the floor to stretch your left quad. Look down or ahead. Hold, lifting your hips and chest on every inhalation. Switch legs.

3 **Full kneeling quad stretch:** Return to kneeling and take your hands behind you, fingers pointing backwards. Lift both hips off the floor. Tuck your tailbone under. Look down or ahead. This pose can also be done statically, or dynamically by lifting on an inhalation and lowering on an exhalation.

4 Half reclining quad stretch: Extend just your right leg along the floor, keeping your left leg in a kneeling position. Sit tall and monitor any discomfort in your left knee. If your knee is comfortable tuck your tailbone under and lower slowly back to rest on your forearms. Exit slowly, pressing onto both hands to rise up evenly. Switch sides.

5 Full reclining quad stretch: Recline back with both legs in a kneeling position, taking care. Keep your tailbone tucked under – if it is accessible – rest on your forearms. Tuck your chin in and stay gazing ahead. Exit slowly, pressing onto both hands to rise up evenly.

6 Quad and hamstring stretch: Straighten just your right leg and lean into a gentle forward bend. You may need to place a block under your right buttock to keep the hips level. Keep your back straight and take your chest – not your nose – towards your knee.

7 Full hamstring stretch: End by shifting out of the position and extending both legs. Tip into a gentle forward bend. If the hamstrings are tight loop a strap around the soles of your feet. Bend your knees if necessary.

THE ADDUCTORS

The adductors, or inner thigh muscles, don't feature in many post-run stretching repertoires, but can become tight after running due to their key leg stabilising role. Aside from the floor-based stretches (such as cobbler's pose) featured here, squatting is a great way to stretch your adductors, as well as the entire groin and hip area and your calves (see previous chapter, page 78).

COBBLER'S POSE

Sit tall, with a block or cushion under your hips if your back rounds. Bring the soles of your feet together. For a stronger version bring your heels closer to your pelvis. Interlace your fingers around your feet and lengthen your spine by lifting from the crown of your head. If your back is rounding sit on a block or grasp higher up, around your ankles. Hold without pressing or bouncing your knees.

SEATED LATERAL STRETCH

This posture is a deeply satisfying whole-body stretch for runners, targeting the adductors, lengthening the hamstrings of your extended leg and releasing built-up tension in the side of the torso from glute medius upwards. From cobbler's pose, extend your right leg out to the side. Point your right toes up. Rest your right hand on your leg, or reach further for your ankle or foot. Place your left hand on your hip and draw your left shoulder back. Breathe in. On an exhale tip into a gentle side-bend over your extended leg. Either gaze ahead or look up. For a deeper lateral stretch sweep your left arm up and over and let it hang.

WIDE-LEGGED FORWARD-BEND

For an adductor/hamstring stretch take your legs wide with your toes pointing upwards. Sit tall with your fingertips resting on the floor. Take note: if you have any back issues, especially a slipped disc, stay high or stick with cobbler's pose. Otherwise walk your fingertips forwards drawing your chest (not your nose) towards the floor. Find a comfortable stretch, then relax your head and breathe deeply.

HALF HAPPY BABY

Half happy baby is basically a supine runner's lunge so a good option for those who can't weight-bear on the back knee. This deep post-run stretch also works into your hamstrings and groin.

Lie on your back. Bend your right leg and place your foot on the floor. Draw the left leg in towards your abdomen but then raise the sole of your foot towards the ceiling. Hold on to your foot and draw it downward, as if encouraging your left knee into your left armpit.

HAPPY BABY

For a full happy baby repeat half happy baby but use both legs. Grip your feet, drawing your knees towards your armpits and rock from side to side to massage your lower back.

THE HIP FLEXORS

The hip flexors (psoas and iliacus), located at the top of the thigh, are one of the runner's hardest working muscle groups, literally lifting the leg on each step. The repetitive action of running can create short, tight hip flexors, leading to potential back problems so don't skimp on stretching. The following post-run lunge sequence is based on runner's lunge. It stretches your hip flexors while easing tension from your quads, iliotibial band, hamstrings, calves and shins.

Post-run lunge sequence

If you only have time for one sequence, this is a fantastic option as it targets every major running tight spot. Take five breaths in each stage of the sequence. Keep your breath flowing slowly during the side-to-side lunge. Or practise the entire sequence in a faster flow. If required pad your back knee by folding the mat over or resting your knee on a cushion or block.

1 Runner's lunge: Start on all fours. Step your right foot up in between your hands and sink into the lunge by dropping your hips. To move deeper ease your back knee further away.

2 Hamstring/shin stretch: Sit back towards your heel so your front leg straightens and you feel your hamstrings lengthening. Press your front foot into the floor.

3 Windscreen wiping: Remain here but roll your front foot onto your heel to stretch your calves. 'Windscreen wipe' your foot from side to side.

4 **Quad stretch lunge:** Shift forward into runner's lunge. Lift your upper body and rest both hands on your front thigh. Tuck your pelvis under and sink your hips a little on each exhalation. Repeat three times dropping gradually lower.

5 **Backbend lunge:** Interlace your hands behind your back and draw them down to open your shoulders. Lift your chest and lean slightly back.

6 **IT band lunge:** Return your upper body to an upright position. Place your right hand on your right leg and sweep your left arm over. Hold, tucking your pelvis under.

7 **Lateral lunge:** Walk your fingertips around so you are facing the side of the room in a wide-legged stance. Start to move side-to-side to stretch your inner thighs. Stay on the soles of your feet or lower right on to your heels, with your toes pointing up.

8 **Runner's lunge (facing the opposite way):** Turn to the back of the room so your left foot is in front and lower into a runner's lunge. Repeat the sequence.

Iliotibial band syndrome

It is nicknamed 'runner's knee', but iliotibial band syndrome (ITBS) isn't really a knee injury, although pain or swelling is felt on the outside of the joint. ITBS occurs when the iliotibial band becomes inflamed and is a common overuse running injury afflicting both novice and seasoned runners. There are numerous causes of this inflammation, including high mileage, overdoing the hill runs or wearing worn out shoes. Another cause is iliotibial band tightness so stretching regularly is thought to help. The only problem is that the iliotibial band doesn't have stretch receptors making it hard to know if you've targeted it correctly. Make the standing IT band stretch a staple, then mix in a range of postures that focus on that outer hip area, such as pigeon and triangle. Combine stretching with regular (beneficial, but excruciating) self-massage by lying on your side on a foam roller and working up and down the outside of the thigh, or invest in regular sports massages. Lengthening the hip flexors, quads and hamstrings may also help prevent ITBS.

THE ILIOTIBAL BAND

The iliotibial band is a thick ligament that runs down the outside of your thigh, from hip to shin and can be the bane of a runner's life if it becomes inflamed (see box opposite). Locating the iliotibial band is not always straightforward, so prevent tightness – a contributing factor to iliotibial band syndrome – by performing a range of stretches and yoga postures that hone in on your outer hip and thigh area.

STANDING ILIOTIBIAL BAND STRETCH

Stand with your feet hip-distance apart. Step your right foot over so your legs are crossed at your ankles. As you inhale sweep your right arm up. On an exhalation, side-bend towards your left and sweep your top arm over.

LYING PIGEON

Lie on your back and hug your right leg into your abdomen. Place your left hand on your knee and extend your right arm along the floor, shoulder-height. Inhale. On an exhalation draw your right knee over to your left. Aim to keep your right shoulder on the floor and turn your head to the right.

Pigeon (page 103), figure four sitting (page 104), seated twist and advanced seated twist (both page 105) also target your outer hip and IT band.

THE GLUTES AND PIRIFORMIS

Don't neglect your glutes, especially if you include sprinting or hill reps in your training schedule. Included in this chapter is a section on piriformis. Some of the following postures, such as pigeon, also stretch the IT band.

Seven steps to pigeon pose

Pigeon is a fantastic all-rounder for runners targeting your glutes, piriformis, ITB, adductors, hip, hamstrings… just about every area that is tight in a runner. Be warned: pigeon can feel intense so inch towards it using the following steps, or substitute lying pigeon pose if your knees and hips won't permit the deep flexion and internal rotation that pigeon requires. Advanced pigeon is reserved for the supple and injury-free runner.

1 **Lying pigeon pose:** As described on page 101.

2 **Runner's lunge:** Move onto all fours, step your right foot up between your hands and sink your hips. Relax your back foot.

3 **Runner's lunge hip stretch:** From runner's lunge heel/toe the right foot out to the right. Place your right hand inside your foot and sink your hips. Feel a strong stretch in your hips and groin. To go deeper, lower onto your forearms.

4 Runner's lunge quad stretch: Only attempt this stage if it is comfortable for the back knee. Rise back to runners lunge, bend the back leg and reach back to hold the foot with your left hand.

5 Gentle pigeon: Revert to runner's lunge and slowly lower your right knee to the floor. Then shuffle your right foot slightly over to your left making sure that your foot is flexed to protect your knee joint. Bend your arms a little, but stay high and watch for any discomfort or pain in your knee joint.

6 Pigeon: If your knee is comfortable and you want to go deeper, lower onto your forearms. Or stack one hand on top of the other and rest your forehead on your top hand. Try to relax into the posture. Ease out slowly.

7 Advanced pigeon: Rise back up to gentle pigeon, bend your back leg and reach one hand back to hold your foot. The back leg should be in contact with the floor just above your kneecap, rather than directly on the joint. To challenge your balance hold onto your back foot first with one hand, then with two.

Piriformis syndrome

Piriformis syndrome is felt either as a pain in the centre of your glutes or down the back of your leg. Like many running injuries the causes are numerous, but overuse is a central one. Piriformis rotates your hip and leg, aids with balance while one foot is off the ground and stabilises your pelvis, making it a hardworking running muscle. Without adequate rest and stretching it can become tight and also irritate the sciatic nerve. As always, a visit to the physiotherapist is required if already suffering from suspected piriformis syndrome, but sitting cross-legged, practising pigeon or lying on your back, crossing your legs at your thighs and drawing them into your abdomen are all good stretches. You could also try perching on a foam roller and making small circles or placing a spikey massage ball against the wall, pressing the centre of your glutes into the ball and making similar rotation movements.

FIGURE FOUR SITTING

The mechanics of this stretch are similar to pigeon, but by inching your legs progressively closer you can very gradually increase the intensity and measure progress. Sit with your legs bent and feet on the floor. Take your hands behind your back, fingers pointing in. Lift your right foot off the floor and turn your knee out. Place your foot on your left thigh and flex it. Now draw your shoulders back and elevate your chest. Breathe slowly. To move deeper shuffle your left foot nearer to your hips and repeat your chest elevation movement. Repeat twice.

SEATED TWIST

Sit in a 90° position with your legs stretched out in front. If it's hard to maintain a tall back, perch on the edge of a block or cushion. Bend your left leg and step your foot over your right thigh. Hold onto your left shin with both hands and sit tall. Wrap your right arm around your left thigh and drop your left fingertips behind you. Inhale, and as you exhale, rotate to your left in sections: lumbar spine, thoracic spine, shoulders and head. Remain here for five breaths. Lift with each inhale and rotate a little further with each exhale. Repeat on your other side.

ADVANCED SEATED TWIST

If your hips are sufficiently supple try advancing the twist. This pose targets the piriformis, erector spinae, rhomboids and neck. Perform the seated twist as before. Now lean to the right and bend your right leg so that the heel of your right foot tucks in next to your left buttock. Level your hips (place a cushion under one hip if it is lower). Wrap your right arm around your left thigh and drop your left fingertips to the floor behind you. Inhale, and as you exhale, rotate to the left. Hold the pose for five breaths. Return to face front and repeat on the other side.

How to sit cross-legged

The basic cross-legged position is called *sukhasana* in Sanskrit, which translates as 'happy', 'sweet', 'easy' or 'blissful', but to many runners it's far from sweet. The reasons for this are various but tight hamstrings, quads and adductors make knee flexion and hip external rotation uncomfortable and prevent your spine lengthening. Throw in the fact that the male pelvis is narrower than the female, restricting this external rotational movement further, and you can see why sitting in sukhasana doesn't feature in any lists of top ten running stretches. So why bother?

SIX CROSS-LEGGED BENEFITS FOR RUNNERS:

1 **Stretches piriformis:** Sukhasana is a simple way to stretch the piriformis, the muscle nestled in the centre of your glutes that can become irritated through running and cycling.

2 **Stretches your groin:** Sukhasana lengthens your adductors, or inner thighs, but also your entire hip and groin area which can easily become tight in runners.

Crossed legs: start with the sofa

If the thought of sitting cross-legged on the floor is a giant step too far, begin by sitting cross-legged on the sofa while watching TV. Position yourself at the rear of the seat with a straight back. Prop the knees with cushions if required. Remember to periodically switch the foot in front to evenly open your hips. The next move is on to the floor with the back resting against the sofa or the surface of a wall. Sit on a cushion or stack them under your knees. If your hips are still distractingly tight, then try cobbler's pose instead with the soles of your feet together. Finally, if you think your cross-legged days are behind you, or you have knee problems, then just opt to sit on a chair. The most important element with mental focus is a straight back so, however you sit, work to elevate your spine.

• **Head:** Stack your head above your torso, tuck your chin slightly in and imagine a puppet string attached to the crown of your head lifting you upwards.

3 **Strengthens your back:** The back muscles, particularly your spinal erectors are strengthened through the action of sitting erect in sukhasana (once your hips have released sufficiently to allow your back to lengthen).

4 **Improves posture:** We saw in Chapter 2 how mountain pose helps improve everyday and running posture. Sukhasana has many of the same benefits: lengthening your spine, aligning your head and drawing back your shoulders.

5 **Breathing base:** Sukhasana is designed to provide a wide, stable tripod-shaped base to enable the student to focus on yoga's many breathing techniques.

6 **Meditation base:** Sitting up straight lets you focus on the workings of the mind without feeling sleepy; a real danger when lying down. But this can only happen when a level of lower body comfort is found.

- **Shoulders:** Draw your shoulders back and down away from your ears. If you still feel tension, squeeze your shoulders under your ears, hold for a few seconds, then release.

- **Arms:** Let your hands rest on your thighs, palms face up to open your shoulders.
- **Chest:** Slightly elevate your chest by lifting your sternum.
- **Abdomen:** Relax your abdomen so it can subtly move in and out as you breathe.
- **Hips:** Perch on the edge of a yoga block or two, or sit on a folded up blanket. This allows your pelvis to tilt forwards, creating a more neutral spine.
- **Knees:** Prop your knees with cushions to support and relax your legs or sit in cobbler's pose with the soles of your feet together.
- **Feet:** Place a sock under your foot as a cushion if there is discomfort from your feet pressing into the floor. Periodically switch your front foot to stretch your hips evenly.
- **Back:** Sit against a wall if your back aches, resting the back of your head against the surface.

POST-RUN HIP SEQUENCE

This hip joint mobilising sequence releases a tight lower back and stretches your hip muscles, glutes and adductors. I begin every yoga for runners session with it because it lets the runner assess levels of tightness in their lower back, hips, hamstrings and ankles. This hip-based sequence works well followed by the all-in-one leg sequence.

Take five to ten breaths in each stage of the sequence.

1 **Lower back releaser:** Lie on your back and hug your right leg into your abdomen. Point your left toes to the ceiling and press the back of your left knee into the mat. Slowly rotate your right foot in small circles.

2 **Hip opener:** Keep your right hand on your right leg and slide your left hand onto your left hip to keep it grounded. Ease your right knee out to your right to stretch your hip and adductors.

3 **Lower back releaser:** Return to the centre.

4 **Lying pigeon:** Place your right palm on the floor and use your left hand to draw your right leg across your body. Turn your head to the right. Extend your right arm along the floor and turn your palm up.

5 **Lower back releaser:** Return to the centre and switch legs.

POST-RUN STRAP SEQUENCE

This is a no-effort stretching sequence after a long, hard run. Just grab a dressing gown belt or old tie, collapse on the grass or living room floor and enjoy a series of deep, relaxing stretches. This restorative sequence speeds up recovery both by inverting your legs, which encourages lymph drainage, and allowing your body to relax into a longer stretch. Reap the rewards of your patience in the form of a smoother, more fluid stride and a greatly reduced chance of injury. Turn to chapter 4 for a standing version of this sequence, balanced stretch (p70).

1 Hamstring and calf stretch:
Lie on your back with your right leg bent, foot on the floor and loop the strap, belt or tie, around your left foot to perform a hamstring stretch. Don't 'lock' your leg straight, especially if your hamstrings are tight. It should be deep but never painful, so if your leg is shaking, ease off. Walk your hands up the strap so you are not straining your arms, rest your shoulders and head on the floor and draw your chin in. After 40 seconds here shift the emphasis to your calves by pointing your toes down and pushing your heel to the ceiling.

2 Adductor/hip stretch:
To target your inner hamstrings, adductors and release tension in your hip take both parts of the strap into your left hand and slowly swing your leg out to your left side. Lift your right leg off the floor and extend your right arm along the floor and look to the right. Stay for 30–60 seconds.

3 Outer hamstring/iliotibial band stretch: Draw your leg back to its original hamstring stretch position. Pass your strap into your right hand and extend your left arm out along the floor. Start by taking the leg just a few inches across the body, keeping the hip grounded. Stay for a few breaths to stretch the iliotibial band and outer hip. Then tip the leg further over and let the hip lift off the floor to target the glutes and enjoy a deeper rotation. Turn the head in the opposite direction.

4 Quad stretch: Keep the strap loosely anchored around your right foot and roll onto your left side. Sweep your arm up and place your palm face down on the floor for balance and as a platform to rest your head. Bend your left leg for support if you are unsteady. Bend the top leg and walk your hand down the strap. Line up your knees and push your hips forward until your quads stretch. This may be enough and if so, stay where you are. To go deeper into the quads and hip flexors draw back the top foot like a bow.

5 Leg hug: End by hugging both legs into your abdomen. Repeat the sequence for your right leg.

07

THE RUNNER'S CORE

❛ I always thought 'core' was just another word for 'abs' and what did the perfect six-pack have to do with running? But core is actually all about strength and stability. Practising yoga has helped me build this deep inner strength and taught me ways to engage it when pounding the pavements, making me a stronger runner and less prone to the same old injuries. ❜

Hannah Dunnell, runner and blogger

(Dunsontherun.com)

A weak core is one of the main reasons runners turn to yoga and its close relative Pilates. Core muscles are recruited heavily in yoga and not only while holding the postures designed specifically to target this area, such as plank (page 122). All of yoga's standing postures require a stable centre to maintain balance or alignment.

This emphasis on the core, in combination with its ability to correct imbalances through stretching, makes yoga ideal for runners. The rewards of a regular practice will be reaped not only in the form of improved running posture but also in balance, speed and power.

THE ROLE OF THE CORE

What is the core?

The term 'core' covers far more than just your abdominals. Yes, the term core does encompass the various layers of abs, but also your lower back and the oft-neglected gluteals. Basically, the core denotes the mid-section of your body, from the tops of your thighs up to your chest.

As runners we want this mid-section to be as stable as possible in order to allow the legs and arms to move freely. A good core session will target all these muscles at the front, back and sides of your torso (details on page 116), and ideally in a running-specific way.

RUNNING-SPECIFIC CORE STRENGTH

Running experts often talk about strength work being 'functional'. This essentially means practising strengthening moves that replicate the running action. Many of the yoga postures in this chapter have been adapted specifically to suit runners. For example running bridge circles the legs in a striding motion, while running planks raise and lower them. Old-style sit-ups that stress your hip flexors and lower back are replaced by movements that work the deep abdominals while maintaining a long, neutral spine, exactly as they would function if you were upright and running.

Four reasons to strengthen your core

1 To run taller

Envisage your core as a corset-like structure that wraps around your torso holding your body erect. If your body's core is weak your spine will collapse and curve, creating rounded shoulders and poor overall posture. This inhibits breathing and creates a heavy footfall as the weight of your head and upper body shifts forwards. Yoga's wide range of strengthening postures will tighten this corset to maintain a balanced upright posture even when your body fatigues.

2 To run faster (and tackle hills)

Gluteus maximus is often omitted from core training sessions, but this thick buttock muscle helps drive your body forwards. Sprinters rely on glute max more than endurance runners,

but a good level of strength in your buttocks – and the entire core – will benefit all runners by allowing the legs to generate more force and speed. The extra power supplied by a strong glute max is especially useful in short sprints or when tackling hills and adds to overall resilience.

3 To limit unnecessary rotation

A key function of the core, especially the internal and external obliques at the sides of your waist, is to minimise upper body rotation in running. This means that your body is moving in an efficient forwards-only motion or sagittal plane rather than swaying from side to side. Restraining this movement creates a more economic stride and saves precious energy for the run.

4 To prevent injury

A weak core can cause numerous problems in runners, from irritating your pelvic muscles to stressing your knee joints or causing nagging lower backache. This is especially the case for runners with sedentary desk jobs who may already have muscular weaknesses in the abdominals and glutes. Of course a strong core is only part of the story with injury prevention; a 'whole-body' strengthening and stretching routine is the ideal preventative solution. Yoga offers this top-to-toe approach but with a constant focus on the core.

The **abdominals** comprise a deep corset-like layer – the transversus abdominis (TVA), 'six-pack' rectus abdominis and two layers of obliques at the sides of the waist. In yoga we are most interested in strengthening the deepest TVA layer rather than toning the superficial (but aesthetically pleasing!) six-pack because of the TVA's postural role. However, because the abs are so interconnected, both groups are engaged in postures like plank. Finally, the internal and external obliques keep the body in alignment as the limbs move in running. Build resilient obliques through the lateral strength sequence (page 127).

The **glutes** are your buttock muscles. The gluteus maximus is one of the thickest muscles in your body and aids with sprinting and hill running.

Postures that target the main gluteus maximus include basic bridge (page 133), locust legs (page 132) and especially running bridge (page 134), which force your glutes to work in isolation just as they do in running. The smaller gluteus medius, at the side of your hips, is frequently overlooked, but has a key role in stabilising your thigh bone. This helps channel all movement into a sagittal motion. Access it by working through the lateral strength sequence (page 127) or just select single leg raises from this series.

Aches in the lower **back** are common in running, especially if training for a long-distance event. Tight hamstrings are often the culprit as they pull your pelvis out of alignment, but yoga's strengthening backbends, along with abdominal work, will reinforce your lower and mid-back so that it is better able to absorb the shock of running. Try locust (page 132), which reinforces your back extensors, releases back/shoulder tension and improves overall running posture. For gentle postures to ease lower backache go to Chapter 11.

Don't forget to breathe

What separates yoga from simple stretching or strength work is breath awareness. Why? Focusing on your breathing keeps your mind on the exercises and stops you pushing beyond your boundaries. Breathing is nasal, slow and relaxed. The core postures in this chapter can either be held *statically* for five (or more) slow breaths, or done *dynamically* in more of a flow. For example, hold plank for five to ten slow breaths. Or inhale in plank, exhale to drop into low plank and inhale back to plank again. Both are valid methods of working and add a little variety into core strengthening.

CORE FOUNDATION POSTURES

The following postures are the building blocks of core work in yoga. These techniques will get you acquainted with the muscles of the core in a gentle, accessible way, explore the function of breathing in strength work and introduce some running-specific movements.

Core foundation postures will also:
- Relieve post-run lower backache
- Engage the deep, stabilising TVA
- Prepare the core for strenuous core exercises
- Provide gentler core options for runners with lower back or abdominal weakness or injury.

THE PELVIC TILT
Targets: TVA and pelvic floor.
Stretches: Lower back.
Running results: Pelvic tilts are a gentle way to release a tight or aching lower back post-run, while engaging the deep abdominals and pelvic floor.
Method: Lie on your back. Bend your legs and place your feet on the floor, hip-width apart. On an inhalation lift your navel keeping your hips grounded to create a gap under your lumbar spine. On an exhalation press your navel into the floor to flatten your lower back. Repeat four times. End by hugging your legs into your abdomen.

CAT
Targets: TVA.
Stretches: The entire back and shoulders.
Running results: Cat eases post-run tightness and lower backache, and gently works your abdominals.
Method: Start on all fours. As you inhale raise your head slightly, and your hips, dipping in your mid back. As you exhale round your back, tucking your chin in and tailbone under. Push your mid-back towards the ceiling and draw your belly in. Repeat four times.

TIGER

Targets: TVA, glutes and hamstrings.
Stretches: Back.
Running results: Tiger trains runners to keep the pelvis stable while the legs move mimicking the running action.

Method: Repeat cat but straighten your left leg and raise it up in line with your hips when you raise your head. As you exhale round your back, tuck your chin in, bend your leg and draw your knee into your abdomen. Repeat four times, then switch legs.

TABLE TOP

Targets: TVA, glutes, hamstrings and back extensors.
Running results: Keeping your torso stable while moving the opposite arm and leg mimics the running action, and improves balance and coordination.

Method: As you inhale raise your left leg and right arm in a diagonal stretch. Remain here gazing downwards for five breaths or transition slowly from side to side aiming to keep the torso still and stable.

Runners' sit-ups sequence

Why *runners'* sit-ups? This core-strengthening sequence is performed largely with your spine in a lengthened, neutral position, to replicate an upright running stance. It uses your abs rather than your hip flexors to draw your body up, in contrast with traditional sit-ups which can overstress this muscle group as well as the neck muscles.

This is good news for runners whose hip flexors are already fatigued from repetitive leg lifting. Approach the sit-ups in stages, holding Stage 1 statically first to gain strength before experimenting with a dynamic rolling up, and lowering down movement. If you have superior abdominal strength (and no lower back weakness) perform all the stages in succession with no rest.

STAGE 1: STATIC LIFT

Lie supine on the floor with your legs together and toes pointing towards the ceiling. Press your lower back into the floor. Interlace your hands behind your head and rest the weight of your head into your hands so your neck muscles relax. Breathe in. As you breathe out lift your head and upper shoulders off the floor

using your abs, not your neck. Remain here for five to ten slow breaths. To advance, try to peel your shoulder blades off the floor.

STAGE 2: STATIC LIFT WITH LEGS

Repeat Stage 1, but for more running realism raise your right leg a few inches off the floor as you breathe in and lower as you breathe out. Switch sides, moving steadily from leg to leg.

STAGE 3: SLOW RISE UP

Sit up and extend your arms in front, interlacing your fingers.
Breathe in. Tuck your chin in. As you inhale keep your chest lifted
and rise slowly up to sitting as if being pulled by your hands.

Visualising the vertebrae

To add another dimension to the lowering and lifting section of the runner's sit-up sequence try visualising. Close your eyes and picture your spine as a string of pearls or a bicycle chain. Now, as you roll down imagine laying each pearl or chain segment down one by one. Repeat the process as you peel your spine back off the floor to rise up. By closing your eyes and picturing your spine you add a depth and mindfulness to the exercise that is the polar opposite of fast, jerky sit-ups of school days.

STAGE 4: LOWERING AND LIFTING

Stay with your hands interlaced. Breathe in. As you breathe out
lower smoothly to the floor. Inhale and rise back up. Repeat four
times. Aim to make the roll-up as fluid as the roll-down.

THE PLANK SERIES

Plank features heavily in yoga, especially in the dynamic sequences used in vinyasa flow, ashtanga and power yoga. In these faster-flowing routines plank is used as a transitional pose to glide between postures. However, plank is a very effective strengthening posture when held statically. Unlike most yoga poses that both build and stretch muscles, plank is a pure strength pose. It improves running power and posture by splinting your torso, and creates upper body strength for an effective arm pumping action. Try the running plank sequence for running-specific variations once you are feeling strong in basic plank.

HIGH PLANK

Targets: TVA, rectus abdominis, arm and shoulder muscles.
Running results: Improved posture and power.
Method: From all fours lift your knees off the floor ensuring the wrists are under your shoulders. Push your heels away, engaging your leg muscles to share the strain. Gaze to the floor and stay for five to ten slow breaths.
Modify: Weak core: drop your knees down, but keep your head, back and hips in line and abdomen engaged. Wrist issues: opt for forearm plank.

LOW PLANK

Targets: Core, chest and arms, especially your triceps.
Running results: Improved posture and upper body power.
Method: From high plank, bend your arms until your elbows fall in line with your torso. Stay for five to ten breaths maintaining alignment.
Modify: Drop your knees down until your arm strength improves.

FOREARM PLANK

Targets: Core, upper back, shoulder and upper arm muscles.

Running results: Improved posture and upper body power. Dropping your centre of gravity forces your core to work harder.

Method: Come onto your forearms, stacking your elbows under your shoulders. Make fists with your hands and keep your forearms parallel, or interlock them. Lift your knees off the floor. Stay for five to ten breaths.

Modify: Drop your knees to the floor, but keep your head, back and hips in line and your abdomen drawn in.

The plank rules

1 Maintain a line along the back of your body from your head to your heels. It is better to drop your knees down and draw your abdomen in to hold onto this alignment, than to sag in your lower back or lift your hips. See modified high plank (page 122).

2 Engage your leg muscles and push your heels away so your lower limbs share the strain.

3 Look down, not ahead, but don't let your head drop. It should continue the line of the spine.

4 Wrist weakness, injury or carpal tunnel syndrome? Opt for a 'forearm' plank or modified forearm plank (above).

5 Any lower back discomfort lie on your back and hug the legs in to the abdomen.

Running planks

The following four planks build sport-specific strength by mimicking the running stride. Each variation shifts the emphasis onto different muscle groups, including your glutes, hip flexors and obliques. Only attempt the running planks when you have mastered good alignment in basic plank.

RUNNING PLANK 1

Targets: Core, arms and the glute maximus.
Running results: The biggest glute provides power and speed.
Method: Perform high plank or forearm plank and lift and lower one leg at a time, keeping your legs straight. Move slowly maintaining level hips. Repeat five times moving from leg to leg.
Modify: Perform the leg raises on all fours.
Advance: As you raise your right leg, also raise your left arm. Exhale back to plank and switch sides. Move slowly side to side or hold.

RUNNING PLANK 2

Targets: TVA, rectus abdominis, hip flexors and arms.
Running results: Creates a 'crunching' action to challenge your core.
Method: Perform high plank. Inhale, and as you exhale, round your back, tuck your chin in and draw your right knee towards your nose. Pause for a second, drawing in your belly. As you inhale return to plank. Repeat on the left side and continue to move from side to side, synchronising the movement and breathing. Repeat five times on each side.
Modify: Perform a gentler version on all fours.

RUNNING PLANK 3

Targets: Glute medius, TVA, rectus abdominis.

Running results: Works the outer hip and thigh which serve to stablise the pelvis as you run.

Method: Perform high plank. Inhale, and as you exhale, bend your right leg out to the side, bringing your knee outside of the right elbow. Pause for a second. As you inhale, return to plank. Repeat on the left side and move side to side synchronising the movement and breath. Repeat five times on each side.

Modify: Perform a gentler version on all fours.

RUNNING PLANK 4

Targets: Obliques, glute medius, TVA , rectus abdominis.

Running results: Stronger obliques achieved through this twisting action mean less unwanted torso rotation in running. Glute medius stablisies the pelvis.

Method: Perform high plank. Inhale, and as you exhale move your right knee under the body, across to the left arm. Pause for a second. As you inhale return to plank. Repeat on the left side and move side to side, synchronising the movement and breath.

RUNNING PLANK 5

Targets: Strengthens your triceps, back, glutes and hamstrings.

Stretches: Pectorals, shoulders and hips.

Running results: This 'reverse plank' is fantastic for improving running posture; it draws back your shoulders and stretches tight pectoral muscles preventing rounded shoulders.

Method: Flip over into a 'table top' position with the belly facing up. Straighten the legs and lift your hips in line with your torso and draw the soles of your feet down towards the floor. Gaze upwards or forward. Don't tip your head back. Take up to five breaths.

Advance: On an inhalation raise your right leg, exhale and lower. Repeat five times moving from leg to leg. Lower down. Make fists with your hands and rotate.

Modify: Wrist injury: avoid this pose. For a gentler version bend your legs so there is less weight on your upper body or try this reverse plank without the leg lift.

LATERAL STRENGTH SEQUENCE

This sequence bolsters your muscles at the side of your torso and hips to prevent excessive side-to-side twisting in running. It will strengthen your entire core, but hones in on your abdominal obliques at the sides of your waist and your lateral hip muscle glute medius which stabilises your pelvis.

SINGLE LEG RAISES

Lie on your right side with your head resting on your hand. Stack your legs on top of each other and line up your legs with the rest of your body. On an inhalation raise your top leg off the floor. Exhale and lower. Repeat five times.

DOUBLE LEG RAISES

Place a hand on the floor for balance and move your legs forwards a little. On an inhalation raise both legs off the floor, exhale and lower. Repeat five times.

SCISSORING

Separate the legs and swing them back and forth in a scissoring motion. Or just swing the top leg. Keep your breath flowing steadily. Continue for five to ten breaths.

MODIFIED SIDE PLANK

Stack your legs back in line with your torso and bend them so your legs form a 90° angle. Rest your weight on your forearm and rest your top arm down the length of your body for extra weight. Stay for five to ten breaths either static or pulsing your hips slightly up and down.

SIDE PLANK

To advance straighten your legs out and rise up into side plank – still resting on your forearm. Either stay static for five to ten breaths, or pulse your hips slightly up and down. Breathe in to lift and out to lower.

SIDE PLANK LEG RAISE

To advance raise your top leg off your lower leg on an inhalation. Hold for up to five breaths.

Repeat this lateral strength sequence on the other side.

RUNNERS' ABS

Supine sequence

This sequence of abdominal exercises isolates your abs in a supine (lying face up) position, replicating a running motion whereby your torso is lengthened, still and stable while your legs move smoothly and freely. Keep the lower back lightly pressed into the floor throughout this sequence. Work slowly, with control, only introducing your arm swing once you have mastered a smooth running legs motion.

1 START POSITION

Lie on your back with your arms by your sides, palms face down. Bend your legs into a 90° position and raise them so your knees stack over your hips and your toes point to the ceiling. Press your lower back slightly into the floor.

2 TOE TAPS

Keeping your back pressing into the floor slowly lower your right foot down on an exhalation and tap your toes lightly on the floor. As you inhale return your leg to 90°. Repeat five times each leg. The slower the better!

3 RUNNING LEGS

Bend your right leg into your abdomen and slide your left leg down so it hovers above the floor. Inhale, draw your left leg in and exhale switch sides. Move slowly side to side, continuing to press your lower back into the floor. Repeat five times on each side.

4 RUNNING LEGS AND ARMS

As you extend your right leg down above your floor sweep your left arm up and back. Exhale and return to centre. Inhale, slide your right leg down and sweep your left arm up. Continue, moving side to side.

5 AB STRETCH

Sweep your arms up and back. Reach to the back of the room and point or flex your feet. Lift your abdomen to stretch your belly.

Leg inversions

This sequence inverts your legs and provides a gentle hamstring and calf stretch making it an ideal gentle post-run workout, but it should only be performed if your legs can comfortably be held at a right angle. Any less than 90° and your hip flexors will be doing the majority of the work, placing pressure on your lower back.

1 LEGS UP

Check if you can comfortably hold your legs at 90°. Place your arms by your sides, palms face down and raise both legs up towards the ceiling. Flex your feet so that your heels push up and toes point down. Press your lower back into the floor. Stay for five to ten breaths.

2 ARMS WIDE

Raise your arms in line with your shoulders, palms face up. Stay for five breaths, ensuring your lower back is pressed into the floor.

3 ARMS ABOVE HEAD

To advance, sweep your arms up over your head and rest them on the floor. Stay for five breaths, ensuring your lower back is pressed into the floor.

4 SINGLE LEG LOWERING

Take your arms back by your sides. Breathe in. As you breathe out lower your right leg and let it hover above the floor. Inhale and return your leg to 90°. Switch from leg to leg. Ensure that your lower back does not lift or arch off the floor at any point. Repeat four times moving from side to side.

5 HUG YOUR LEGS

Bend your legs and hug them into your abdomen. Rock from side to side.

Warning! Double leg lifts

Be wary of double leg lifts, or raising both legs off the floor from a lying position. This exercise places a huge amount of pressure on your lower back and resulting back injuries are not uncommon. I also don't recommend it for runners because it heavily recruits your hip flexors, rather than your abs, to elevate your legs, a group of muscles already overworked by running. Opt instead for single leg lifts with your lower back pressed into the floor and arms by your side, (see above) or keep one leg bent into your abdomen while you extend the other and let it hover a few inches (or higher) above the floor (see 'running legs' from the supine sequence on page 129).

BACK STRENGTHENERS

Don't forget the lower and mid-back – it's all part of the core. That corset-like protection wraps all the way around the torso. Strong back muscles will aid posture and – together with stretching – minimise that nagging lower backache caused by running and prolonged periods of sitting at work.

Follow backbends like locust pose with a gentle forwards bend to let the back muscles stretch and relax. Extended child (see page 210) is ideal and offers a welcome back and shoulder stretch after a long run. Come to all fours. As you breathe out sit slowly back on your heels. Extend both arms out in front and press your palms into the floor. For a deeper feeling of spinal decompression, inch your fingertips forwards and draw your hips back, in the opposite direction.

LOCUST POSE

Targets: Erector spinae, glutes and hamstrings.
Running results: Locust bolsters the entire back of your body – from your hamstrings to your upper back – improving running posture and overall strength.
Upper body method: Lie face downwards with your arms by your sides. On an inhale keep your legs grounded, but raise your torso and arms, spreading your fingers. Remain looking down. Stay for five slow breaths, then lower down and sit back in extended child.

Whole body method: For the full locust pose, repeat as above, but raise your legs off the floor. Take five slow breaths, then lower down and sit back in extended child.

LOCUST LEGS

Targets: Glute maximus, hamstrings and lower back.
Running results: The glutes provide the explosive boost required to speed up and tackle hills.
Method: Lie face downwards with your arms

close by your sides, palms down. Inhale and raise just your right leg off the floor, keeping your leg straight and your hips grounded and level. Exhale and lower. Repeat four times. Switch to your left leg. Rise slowly up to all fours and sit back in extended child.

The bridge series

Runners are often tight in the hips, so postures like bridge that open the front of the body are ideal. Bridge is also an 'anti-slouch' posture, lengthening tight pectoral muscles and drawing back the shoulders. On the strengthening side, it targets your back, glutes, quads and your hamstrings, especially if your feet are inched further away. Play with the 'running' bridges for a sport-specific focus.

BASIC BRIDGE

Targets: Gluteus maximus, quads and hamstrings.

Stretches: Hip flexors, pectoralis muscles and shoulders.

Running results: Improves running posture and powers the legs.

Method: Lie on your back with the legs bent and feet on the floor, hip-distance apart. Take the arms by your sides, palms face down. On an inhale press the palms into the floor and raise the hips up. Ensure the knees stay aligned with

the hips and don't sway out or inwards. Tuck the chin in. Stay for five to ten breaths, maintaining lift, or work dynamically, inhaling to lift up, and exhaling to lower down.

HAMSTRING BRIDGE

Targets: Hamstrings, quads and glutes.

Running results: Runners need to have supple and strong hamstrings for injury prevention.

Method: Prepare to perform basic bridge, but move your feet further away. On an inhale press your palms into the floor and raise your hips up. Ensure your knees stay aligned with your hips. Tuck your chin in. Stay for five breaths maintaining lift, or work dynamically, by inhaling to lift and exhaling to lower.

Slower is tougher

Bounce rapidly in and out of any core work and you are relying on momentum rather than the abs. Try slowing down to work more deeply. If holding postures for five to ten breaths make them long, deep ones as opposed to counting '1, 2, 3' in rapid panting breaths. Dynamic core work is also twice as tough when done in double the time. For example, slow down your out-breath as you lower down from bridge pose to challenge the deep abdominals, or transition slowly from leg to leg in single leg lifts rather than pumping the legs in a quick scissoring action.

RUNNING BRIDGE 1

Targets: The glutes, quads and hamstrings.

Running results: This bridge variation forces your glutes to work dynamically and in isolation, as they would in running when switching from foot to foot.

Method: Perform bridge. Shift your weight onto your right foot and slowly raise your left leg off the floor, keeping it bent. Lower your foot gradually down and switch sides. Work slowly, shifting from foot to foot. Repeat five times on each side.

Advance: Move more slowly, maintaining lift in your hips.

RUNNING BRIDGE 2

Targets: The glutes, quads and hamstrings.

Running results: This bridge variation forces glute maximus to work in isolation, strengthening one side at a time. The straight leg adds extra weight.

Method: Perform bridge. Shift your weight onto your right foot and slowly raise your left leg off the floor, straightening it so that both thighs are level. Hold for five breaths maintaining lift. Lower down and switch legs.

Advance: To further mimic a running motion, sweep the opposite arm up and back.

LOWER AB SEQUENCE

The block sequence

Squeezing a block between your inner thighs during core work shifts the emphasis to your lower abdominals and pelvic floor while reinforcing your inner thighs, often a weak spot for runners. If you don't own a foam yoga block use a small cushion or rolled up running top.

Lie on your back and place the block between your thighs. Squeeze it by engaging your inner thighs and pelvic floor and sustain this pressure throughout.

1 Legs up: Elevate your legs to a 90° angle. Less than 90°? Bend your legs into a right angle to avoid stressing your lower back or hip flexors. Keep your arms by your sides, palms face downwards. Press your lower back slightly into the floor. Take five to ten breaths.

2 Forward reach: Breathe in and sweep your arms up overhead. Breathe out, reach forwards and peel your head and shoulders off the mat. Repeat four times.

3 Block crunch: Interlace your hands behind your head and lower it to the floor. Bend your legs, but keep your knees stacked over your hips. Breathe in. As you breathe out raise the head and shoulders off the floor. Hold and squeeze. Exhale and lower back down. Work slowly, avoiding a bouncing momentum. Repeat four times.

4 Lower down: Ensure your lower back is pressing into the floor and take four breaths to gradually lower your legs down to the floor.

5 Block bridge: Breathe in and lift your hips towards the ceiling. Exhale and lower down. Repeat four times.

6 Inner thigh stretch: Release the block. Take your arms by your sides, palms down or rest your hands on your belly. Bring the soles of your feet together and let your knees fall out to the sides. Take a few breaths, then draw your knees together and hug your legs into your abdomen.

Work the core standing up

The techniques in this chapter have all been floor-based, but the core can also be strengthened standing up. Step the feet hip-distance apart. Sweep both arms up above the head, interlink the fingers and turn the palms to the ceiling. Breathe in and as you breathe out tip the upper body to the right. Remain here breathing steadily. Stay in the side bend, but release your left hand and feel the muscles of at the side of the waist (the obliques) contracting to hold you in position. This simple side bend is just one way to strengthen the core while upright. For more examples turn to the lateral strengtheners section in the next chapter.

RUNNERS' POWER YOGA

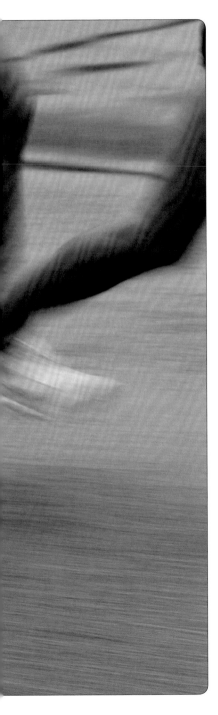

' *Yoga can be just as effective as weights when it comes to building a stronger physique.* **'**

Nicholas DiNubile, orthopaedic surgeon
and sports medicine specialist, USA

Think 'yoga', think 'flexibility'? We know that yoga is fantastic for lengthening tight, hard-working running muscles. Less well known is its strengthening role. Poses such as plank, downward facing dog and the standing postures highlighted in this chapter (such as side angle pose, triangle or warrior 1) are the yogic equivalent of a gym session, but use just your body weight as resistance. No equipment or expensive gym membership is required; just enough space to step your legs out wide or drop to the floor and start working.

WHY DO RUNNERS NEED TO BE STRONG?

The consensus among running experts is that runners who only run risk injury. The body absorbs two to three times its own weight on each foot strike, and strength or resistance sessions create resilient muscles able to absorb and disperse this impact mile after mile. Strength work also has obvious benefits for sprinting, short bursts of acceleration and ascending hills.

Some of the postures in this chapter, such as chair, are pure strength exercises. Chair – a high squat – is a static pose, working your quads and glutes in a straightforward manner. Most standing yoga poses, however, are far more complex...

MUSCLE STRENGTH AND LENGTH

One key difference with yoga is its ability to both strengthen and lengthen muscles thus creating a lean physique. Muscles contract eccentrically (stretch as they contract) to create elongated fibres. This is the opposite of weight training where the fibres contract concentrically to create a compact appearance.

This makes yoga ideal for runners who want to get stronger without creating muscle bulk that would add weight and constrict a fluid stride. Take the triangle pose: the oblique abdominals at the sides of the waist are being stretched, but also working hard to brace your torso over your legs and maintain balance. A runner who is both

supple and strong will double her chances of avoiding injury as resilient muscles stabilise the joints and reduce wear and tear.

WHOLE-BODY TECHNIQUES

Unlike gym machines, which tend to isolate muscle groups, yoga's standing postures are also likely to be challenging many areas simultaneously. Add to that the fact that steady, deep breathing and mental concentration are required for balance and this really makes them whole-body techniques.

A classic example of this is revolved triangle, a twisting, asymmetrical standing posture that demands a high level of strength, flexibility and focus. We approach it in stages in this chapter (Six steps to revolved triangle, page 150 and pictured below), as most runners will find it challenging, but, once mastered, it is a fantastic 'whole body' posture for runners. Let's break down the benefits:

- Strengthening: erector spinae group, internal and external obliques, glute medius and minimus, quadratus femoris, piriformis and the muscles of the feet.
- Stretching: latissimus dorsi, hamstrings, gastrocnemius and soleus and glute medius and maximus, tensor fascia latae and the iliotibial band.
- Balance and proprioception: to hold revolved triangle steady.
- Mental concentration: to maintain balance and precision.
- Breathing awareness: to aid with balance and concentration.

For those unfamiliar with the Latin names of muscles, let's just say there's not much of the body not involved in performing revolved triangle, from your feet (rapidly contracting and releasing to maintain balance) to your neck muscles (rotating your head to look upwards).

When to power up your yoga

The end of your longest run is not the best time to launch into strong standing postures. The foot, leg and hip muscles are already fatigued and require inverting or static stretching to gently restore them to resting length. Instead tag stronger sequences involving squats and lunges on to the end of a light run or practise on rest days. If you race, the off-season is a good time to focus on improving both flexibility and power using some of these stronger postures, so think about upping the intensity of your yoga practice through the winter. If you have time, join a power yoga or ashtanga class, but take note: the pace of these classes is fast and strenuous for novice yogis. If you are totally new to yoga, practise alignment at home first so you have a good basic knowledge of the postures, and rest in class when you need to. Despite what the yogis say these classes can get competitive! It's easy to get caught up and force your body to push beyond its natural limitations.

RUNNING-SPECIFIC STRENGTHENING

Some postures, such as the warrior 1 lunge, mimic a large stride, making them highly suitable for runners. This kind of running-specific or 'functional' strength training is ideal, training the same muscles you use to pound the road or traverse the trails. The variations of warrior 1, such as the balancing warrior or leaning lunge, hold the basic leg stance to strengthen your quads and glutes while stretching your hip flexors, calves or soles of your feet. They can be done statically or as part of a dynamic sequence (see leg power flow, page 160).

STATIC OR DYNAMIC?

A dynamic sequence in yoga links postures together in a flowing routine. A classic example of this is the sun salutation – a series of forward and backbends – that is explored later in this chapter (see page 156). Athletes tend to be drawn to this type of yoga because of its faster pace.

TYPES OF STRENGTH TRAINING

Moving constantly in and out of postures dynamically strengthens the muscles isotonically as they are alternately contracting and releasing. Hold the postures statically and you are working isometrically as the muscle length stays the same. While a flow sounds more fun, static strength work can be just as challenging. Try holding extended triangle or plank for two minutes to really appreciate this! An ideal way to approach the more powerful postures is to study them statically first to work on precision, then speed them up in a flow.

LEG POWER POSES

The following postures will strengthen your quads, hamstrings and glutes for running speed and power. No leg press machine required!

Chair pose

Chair pose translates as 'fierce pose' in Sanskrit, and after a few minutes you'll feel the burn in your quads, hamstrings and glutes. Experiment with your arms by sweeping them up and parallel, interlace your hands behind your head or rest your palms on your hips. As with all the stronger poses, breathe slowly through your nose. Sink lower to increase the intensity. Hold statically for five to ten breaths, or maintain the leg position and transition from one variation to the next.

BASIC CHAIR

Targets: Ankles, quads, hamstrings, glutes, back muscles and triceps.

Stretches: Calves.

Running results: Strengthens the larger leg muscle groups for speed and power and the foot and ankle muscles to absorb the impact of running.

Method: Stand in mountain pose with your feet together. On an inhale sweep both arms up alongside your ears and spread your fingers wide. On an exhalation bend your knees and sink into a high squat. Tuck your tailbone under. Gaze ahead or up to your hands.

Modify: Knee injury: remain in a high squat. Sore or stiff upper back or shoulders: place your hands on your hips.

Advance: Sink lower.

BALANCING CHAIR

A fantastic variation for runners; balancing chair strengthens your shins, calves, ankles and fine muscles of your feet, while improving balance. Perform chair, but rise slowly onto the balls of your feet. Gaze upwards or directly ahead.

TWISTING CHAIR

The rotational movement in twisting chair stretches the torso, squeezing out torso and upper body tension. Reduce the twist if you have lower back problems or sink lower and rotate further to go deeper.

Join your palms in a prayer position. On an exhalation lower into chair then turn your upper body to the left keeping your knees level. To come deeper into the pose, sink low enough to anchor your right elbow to the outside of your left knee. This will give you the leverage to twist further. Repeat on the other side.

ADVANCED TWISTING CHAIR

This advanced version demands a supple torso and good glute/quad strength. Repeat twisting chair. Once in the rotation drop your right fingertips to the outside of left right foot and raise your left arm up. Spread your fingers and turn your head to gaze at your upper hand. To exit, reverse the steps one by one. Repeat on the other side.

WALL CHAIR

To build postural strength and intensify the leg work perform a version of chair with your back and head resting against a wall. Simply stand with your feet hip-distance apart and slide down the wall until your legs form a right angle shape. Rest your hands lightly on your thighs and gaze ahead.

Stick pose

Running can create overdeveloped outer quads and underdeveloped inner quads. This thigh imbalance can lead to potential knee problems.

Tight hamstrings will prevent your spine lengthening, so if your back is rounding sit on the edge of a yoga block or cushion.

Sit with your legs stretched out in front and close together. Straighten your back by lifting from the crown of your head and pressing your palms lightly into the floor. To activate your inner thighs push your knees into the floor and hold for five to ten breaths.

STICK POSE SEQUENCE

1 **Stick pose:** Adopt this pose as described above, and stay for five breaths.

2 **Stick heel lift:** Remain in stick but lift your heels off the floor. Stay for a further five breaths.

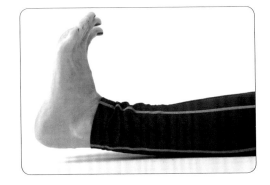

3 Stick leg raises: As you inhale raise your right leg a few inches off the floor keeping it straight, exhale and lower. Move from leg to leg. Repeat four times on each side.

4 Core stick: Move your palms further forwards, push into the floor and lift your hips off the surface. Round your back a little and gaze at your knees. To advance raise your legs off the floor too and hover. Stay for five breaths.

5 Reverse plank: Move your hands behind your hips, fingertips pointing away. Press into the floor. Lift your chest and draw your shoulders back. Stay for three to five breaths.

Make fists with your hands and rotate to release any wrist tension.

THE LUNGES

Lunges mimic a wide stride making them a staple power yoga move for runners. They simultaneously strengthen key running muscles like the quads and hamstrings, and lengthen tight hip flexors, calves and the soles of the feet, depending on the variation. The postures in this section are based on the basic yoga lunge warrior 1. Try holding the lunges statically, or link them together in the leg power flow (page 160) or flying warrior slow flow sequence (page 164).

WARRIOR 1

Targets: Quads, hamstrings and adductors.
Stretches: Hip flexors and calves.
Running results:
Strengthens the quads and hamstrings for accelerating and sprinting power and injury prevention. Restores the calf muscles back to their resting length.

Method: From the middle of your mat take a good step back with your left foot. Turn your back foot slightly out and bend your front knee until it is stacked over your ankle. Take your hands to your hips. Stay for five to ten breaths drawing your back heel to the floor.

Modification: If you have knee problems, perform a higher lunge and ensure the knee of your front leg is behind or stacked above your ankle.
Advance: Sink lower and deepen the backbend. Raise the arms up to shoulder-height and bent into right angles. Lean the torso slightly back.

FLYING LUNGE

Targets: Quads and hamstrings.
Stretches: Hip flexors, calves, chest and shoulders.
Running results: Leaning over the front leg forces the front quad to work harder for extra running power and speed. The 'flying arm' position releases upper body tension and draws back the shoulders.
Method: From the middle of the mat take a good step back with your left foot. Rise on to the ball of your back foot and bend your front knee until it is stacked over your ankle. Lean your torso over your leg:

1 **Arms forwards:** Reach both arms forwards and parallel. Spread your fingers. Stay for five breaths.

2 Arms back: Sweep your arms back and – if your shoulders allow – interlace your fingers. Stay for five breaths.

Modification: For knee problems, perform a higher lunge.

Advance: Shuffle your back foot further back and sink down until your front thigh is parallel with the floor.

TWISTING LUNGE

Targets: Quads, hamstrings and glutes.

Stretches: Hip flexors, calves, torso, back and shoulders.

Running results: Releases hip tension and creates a supple torso to facilitate deeper breathing.

Method: Drop both hands to the floor either side of your feet as if performing a high runner's lunge. As you inhale sweep your right arm up to the ceiling, turning your head to follow your hand. Exhale as you return your arm by your side. Repeat with the other arm, moving from side to side with each breath. Repeat four times on each side.

Modification: For tired legs, drop your back knee to the floor into a lower runner's lunge position.

Six steps to revolved triangle

Revolved triangle is a gem for runners as it targets the majority of a runner's tight spots, especially the iliotibial band, hamstrings and hips. It also improves balance and mental focus. The full posture demands a good level of whole-body flexibility, but by following these steps a sense of revolved triangle should be accessible to all. Avoid this posture if you have lower back problems, such as a slipped disc.

Hold the static positions for five breaths.

1 TWISTING LUNGES

Perform a high runner's lunge. As you inhale sweep your left arm to the ceiling. Exhale return your arm by your side. Repeat with your right arm. Repeat four times on each side.

2 90° HAMSTRING STRETCH

Step up to your hands and slide both hands up to rest just above your knees. Create a 90° shape. Tuck your tailbone in to minimise your lumbar curve. Look downwards.

3 HALF PYRAMID

Begin with your feet hip-width and step your right foot back. Keep the toes of both feet facing front. Sweep your arms behind your back and hold onto your elbows. On an exhalation forward-bend to a 90° position. Maintain a long, straight spine.

4 FULL PYRAMID

Repeat half pyramid but release your fingertips all the way down to the floor, placing them either side of your feet. If they don't reach the floor, bend your front leg or place a block – or stack of books – under each hand. Release your head.

5 HALF REVOLVED TRIANGLE

Take your left hand to your hip. Slide your right hand to the outside of your left leg – knee height is a good place to start. Rotate your upper body to the left. Pause here and see how the posture feels.

6 REVOLVED TRIANGLE

To move deeper slide your right hand further down your left leg and extend your left arm up to the ceiling. Spread your fingers wide. To exit reverse the process, exiting one step at a time. Finally, from 90° hamstring stretch, bend your knees and rise up to mountain pose.

STANDING LATERAL STRENGTHENERS

Running is a very linear sport, which means the hip and leg muscles responsible for sideways or lateral movement can become weakened. These lateral strengtheners redress that imbalance by strengthening the abductors (outer thigh muscles that 'abduct', or take the legs wide) and adductors (inner thigh muscles that draw them together). Also targeted in this section is glute medius and the obliques; these core muscles, located down the sides of the torso and hips, play a key role in minimising rotation during running and benefit greatly from the dual strengthening and stretching that standing postures like triangle or side angle pose offer.

Hold each posture for five to ten breaths.

WARRIOR 2

Targets: Quads and hamstrings.
Stretches: hip flexors, adductors and calves.
Running results: Shifts the body into a lateral plane creating balanced strength.
Method: Turn sideways on the mat and step your feet wide apart. Turn your right foot out 90° and left foot slightly inwards. Bend your front leg ensuring the knee is stacked behind or above the ankle. Raise both arms up to shoulder height, palms face down. Gaze to the front fingertips.
Modify: Knee issues: don't sink too low.
Advance: Shuffle the back foot further away and sink the hips lower until the front thigh is parallel to the ground.

SIDE ANGLE POSE

Targets: Quads, hamstrings and obliques.
Stretches: the entire side of the body
Running results: Increased lateral strength provides power and stability.
Method: Inhale in Warrior II and, as you exhale, bend your right leg and lean into a side bend, resting your right forearm lightly on your front thigh. Tip your left arm over by your ear so that there is a straight line running from your back heel to your top fingertips.
Modify: Knee issues: Perform a higher version with a narrower stance.
Advance: Drop the right fingertips to the outside of the front foot and 'brace' the legs by pushing the right knee into the right elbow. Gaze upwards.

REVERSE WARRIOR

Targets: Quads and hamstrings.

Stretches: obliques, hip flexors and calf.

Running results: The sidebending movement releases muscular tightness in the torso helping facilitate deeper breathing.

Method: Inhale in Warrior 2. On an exhale sweep the front arm up and reach to the ceiling as if performing a wide-legged tennis serve. Slide the back arm down the back leg.

Modify: The combined side/back bend action of reverse warrior can compress the lower back. Rise up and limit the bend.

Advance: Widen the leg stance by shuffling the back foot away until the front thigh is parallel with the floor.

TRIANGLE

Targets: Obliques and glute medius.

Stretches: the entire side of the body including tensor fascia lata and the iliotibial band.

Running results: A staple yoga pose for runners. Triangle both strengthens the lateral muscles that limit excessive rotation and stretches many of a runner's tightest spots.

Method: From Warrior 2, straighten the front leg and tip into a side bend. Drop the right hand to rest lightly on the front thigh and reach the left arm up.

Modify: Limit the side bend, slightly bend the front knee and place the top hand on the hip.

Advance: Step the legs wider and tip the top arm over by the ear.

Triangle and the core

Make your oblique abdominals work harder in triangle by either taking the weight out of your lower hand or even letting it hover just in front of your leg, palm facing outwards. This forces your abs take the strain. Alternatively, take the pressure off the core by resting your hand on your lower leg and enjoying a deep lateral stretch. I like to do both: 'core' triangle for five to ten breaths, followed by a lengthening version, sometimes with my back against the wall to focus solely on the stretching sensation without worrying about strength or balance. A final variation of triangle is to take your top hand to your waist and twist the pose by turning your chest and abdomen towards the ceiling rotating your head to look up. Experiment with this beneficial posture to see which variation suits you.

HORSE

Targets: Glutes, inner thighs.

Stretches: The hips and inner thighs.

Running results: Works the adductors and inner quads – a common weak spot for both runners and cyclists.

Method: Step your feet wide and turn your toes slightly out. Place your hands on your hips or extend your arms out to the side. Tuck your pelvis slightly under. Inhale. On an exhalation bend your knees and come into a high squat so your knees track with the second toe. Don't let your knees collapse inwards.

Modification: For knee issues, perform a higher squat.

Advance: For a deeper squat try horse into squat (opposite).

HORSE INTO SQUAT (AND BACK)

Horse into squat is a powerful strengthening/ stretching combination for runners that also lengthens the calves and challenges the sense of balance. Avoid this technique if you suffer with knee problems.

Begin in horse stance, ensuring your knees track in line with your second toe. Raise your arms up in front and parallel. Let your breath flow freely and begin to sink down in sections. As you near the floor, drop your fingertips down. Pause here and sway your body from side to side. To reverse, raise your arms up again and work up slowly to standing. Take three to four breaths to sink and three to four to rise up; the slower you move, the stronger the work. Repeat four times.

HORSE LATERAL STRENGTHENER

Extend your arms out shoulder-height, palms face up. Breathe in. As you breathe out tip to your right side, resting your forearm on your leg, and sweep your left arm over. Inhale to the centre and exhale to the left.

Advance: Drop your fingertips to the outside of your right heel. Repeat six times.

RUNNER'S FAST FLOWS

Runner's sun salutation

A sun salutation is a series of forward and backward bends practised in quick succession to heat up your body and forge a supple but strong physique. The appeal of this dynamic sequence to runners is clear; it is fast paced and physical compared to static stretching. Sun salutations are also highly versatile. They can be used as a cool-down sequence post-run, or to build strength on rest days. This might be done by pausing in plank for ten breaths, flipping into side plank or stepping up into a balancing lunge.

The runner's sun salutation is a variation of a basic salutation with an extra focus on stretching the calves, hamstrings, hip flexors and quads. Practise it a few times to get the feel of the sequence and breathing (see box opposite) and then concoct your perfect salutation by adding in extra stretches or strength options from the suggestions provided.

Repeat at least twice, alternating the 'stepping back' leg in stage 4.

Stand in mountain pose with your feet together and arms by your sides.

1 **Inhale:** Sweep your arms out and up, bringing your palms together. Lengthen your spine. Extend your spine. **Arching mountain**.

2 **Exhale:** Bend your knees and come slowly into a forward-bend. **Standing forward-bend**.

3 **Inhale:** Rise up halfway, making a right angle of your body and sliding your hands to your knees. **90° stretch**.

'Inhale ... exhale ...'

The tricky element for those new to flow yoga is learning to synchronise the breath and movement. For instance, you inhale as you spread the arms wide in mountain pose, and exhale into a standing forward-bend, inhale, rise to fingertips… this system of breathing continues through the entire sequence. The focus on breathing is what differentiates yoga from pure stretching or strength work; your mind is engaged as it is forced to concentrate on the rhythm of respiration. At some stage this transforms the sequence from a purely physical one into a kind of moving meditation. This shift from mechanical to mindful takes time, but will eventually become totally automatic. A sign that you've reached this stage is practising the entire sequence with your eyes closed.

4 Exhale: Step back into a **high runner's lunge**.

5 Inhale: Sweep one arm up, turning your head. **Twisting lunge**.

6 Exhale: Return to **runner's lunge**.

7 Inhale: Sweep the other arm up, turning your head. **Twisting lunge**. Repeat twice.

8 Exhale: Return to **runner's lunge**.

9 Inhale: Step back to **plank**.

10 Exhale: Lower slowly to the floor keeping your body in line. Make a right-angle shape with your arms as you lower. **Low plank**.

11 Inhale: Press into the floor and raise your upper body into a gentle backbend. **Cobra**.

12 Exhale: Turn your toes under and sit back on your heels, stretching your arms out in front. **Extended child** (foot stretch).

13 Inhale: Rise to **all fours**.

14 Exhale: Lift up into down dog. Stay for four breaths bending one leg and drawing your other heel down. Switch side to side. **Walking dog**.

15 Inhale: Look to your hands, bend your legs and step up in-between your hands. **High lunge**.

16 Exhale: Step your back leg up between your hands and perform a forward-bend. **Standing forward-bend**.

17 Inhale: Bend your knees and rise up to standing. Sweep your arms up above, bringing your palms together. Extend your spine. **Arching mountain**.

18 Exhale: Return your arms to your sides. **Mountain pose**.

VARYING THE SALUTATION

Adapt the basic runner's sun salutation to strengthen the core and/or improve posture by mixing in the following techniques:

Core strength

Pause in plank (step 9) and perform:

- glute plank
- forearm plank
- forearm side plank.

Upper body strength

Pause in dog (step 14), then transition into plank and back to dog five times (inhaling into plank and exhaling back to dog).

Running posture

Lower to the floor (step 10), and try:

- locust
- snake.

Leg power flow

Gain the power to sprint uphill or accelerate to the finish line with this leg-strengthening sequence. A runner who is both supple and strong will also avoid injury, as resilient muscles stabilise the joints and reduce ligament wear and tear. These balances and lunges work the foot, ankles, quadriceps, hamstrings, glutes and hip flexors. Practise on a non-training day or after a light run.

1 **Inhale:** Stand in mountain pose with your feet together and arms by your side. Sweep both arms out at shoulder height. **Standing backbend**.

2 **Exhale:** Lower into a forward-bend, bending your knees as much as required to line up your fingertips and toes. **Forward-bend**.

3 **Inhale:** Slide both hands up your shins to your knees, turning your body into a right angle. **Right angle**.

4 **Exhale:** Step your left leg back into a lunge, dropping your fingertips to the floor either side of your toes. **Runner's lunge**.

5 Inhale: Balancing on the ball of your back foot, slowly rise up into a balancing lunge. Place your hands on your hips, or interlace behind your head, and gaze ahead. Stay for four slow breaths, pushing your hips forward. **Balancing lunge**.

6 Exhale: Let your back knee dip down a few inches above the floor (higher if you have a knee injury). Inhale and rise back up. Repeat three more times. **Lunging dips**.

7 Inhale: Sweep your arms back like wings and spread your fingers. Lean your weight over your front leg. Stay for four breaths, feeling your front quads working. **Leaning lunge**.

8 Exhale: Shift your weight onto your front foot. Slowly raise your back foot off the ground and tilt forwards. Point your back toes down. Stay for four breaths. **Flying warrior 3**.

9 Inhale: Slowly sweep your arms in front and parallel with your palms facing. Stay for two to four breaths. **Full warrior 3**.

10 Exhale: Lower your back foot down as you return to runner's lunge, dropping your fingertips either side of your toes. **Runner's lunge**.

11 Inhale: Step your left foot up next to your right and slide both hands up your shins to your knees, turning your body into a right angle. **Right angle**.

12 Exhale: Lower into a forward-bend, bending your knees as much as required to line up your fingertips and toes. Release your head. **Forward-bend**.

13 Inhale: Bend your knees and draw in your abdomen. As you inhale rise to standing. Sweep both arms out at shoulder height. Return your arms by your side. Repeat the sequence using your right leg. **Standing backbend**.

Dancing warrior

Link warrior 2, side angle pose and reverse warrior in this flowing sequence, called dancing warrior. Lateral techniques like this benefit runners by breaking them out of a linear, or sagittal, plane of motion. The leg position remains static throughout, ensuring the legs get simultaneously strengthened and lengthened while the upper body moves. Dancing warrior is also an excellent core strength technique, forcing the obliques to sway the torso back and forth. Keep your legs firm, but relax the upper body and arms.

1 Inhale: Warrior 2.

2 Exhale: Side angle pose.

3 Inhale: Warrior 2.

4 Exhale: Reverse warrior.
To advance the sequence drop your fingertips to the floor behind your front foot in side angle pose.

RUNNER'S SLOW FLOWS

For a real mental and physical challenge transition between yoga's stronger postures in tai chi-style slow motion. The muscles are forced to hold a pose for longer while the mind fights the urge to rush the sequence. In this sense slow motion flows are good mental training; they encourage present moment awareness. Simply observe the breath and muscles contracting and releasing. I have chosen two slow flows that focus on leg strength and balance.

Flying warrior

STEP 1

Warrior 1: Step your right leg up into a wide lunge and bend your knee until it is behind, or directly over your ankle. Lift the back heel so you are balancing on the ball of the foot. Sweep your arms up and parallel, palms facing. Spread your fingers wide.

STEPS 2 and 3

Flying warrior: In slow motion begin to lean over your front leg and sweep your arms behind you like wings. Continue to shift your body weight onto your front foot until just the tips of your back toes are on the floor.

STEPS 4, 5 and 6

Warrior 3: Simultaneously begin to lift your back leg as you slowly sweep your arms, first to the sides, like a tightrope walker, then in front and parallel with your palms facing.

REVERSE THE SEQUENCE
Still moving in slow motion:
- Float your arms back by your sides like wings in flying warrior.
- Lower your back toes to the floor. Shift half your body weight onto your back foot and sweep your arms up into warrior 1.

How to breathe in slow flows

Rather than syncing breath and movement the idea in slow flows is the keep the breath moving smoothly throughout. The slower and deeper this continual ebb and flow of breath, the better, as this will keep the mind calm and fight any feelings of mounting impatience. You might even experiment with a soothing breathing technique called ocean breath (see page 213), which involves slightly constricting the throat so the breath makes an audible wave-like sound. It should take at least five slow breaths to transition from one posture to another, but slow it down as much as you like. There's only one golden rule in a slow flow: don't rush!

Lateral slow flow

- **Warrior 2:** Step your legs wide. Turn your right foot to face the front of the room and the left foot slightly inwards. Bend your front leg so your knee is behind or stacked over your ankle. Sweep your arms up to shoulder-height, palms face downwards and gaze to your front fingertips.

- **Side angle pose:** Start to lean over your front knee and drop your right fingertips to the floor (or rest your right forearm on your front thigh). Tip your top arm over by your ear.

- **Half-moon:** Don't stop in side angle pose. Continue to crawl your fingertips forward until your weight shifts onto your front leg. Drop your top hand to your waist **(4)** and slowly raise your back leg up while straightening your front leg **(5)**. If balanced, raise your top arm up and spread your fingers **(6)**. Rotate your head and abdomen to gaze momentarily at your fingertips.

REVERSE THE SEQUENCE

- Take your top hand back to your waist, turn your head to look down.
- Lower your back leg, bend your front leg and sweep your arms up to shoulder height, palms face down into warrior 2.
- Straighten both legs and turn to the back of the mat to repeat lateral slow flow with your left foot in front.

09

MENTAL TRAINING

' It amazes me how little time people spend on mental training. 30K into a marathon on race day is too late to figure out you need to train your brain. '

Chrissie Wellington, World Ironman Champion

www.chrissiewellington.org

You've pounded the pavements, strengthened your core and stretched your legs, but what are you thinking? Runners invest years honing the physical body, often forgetting the biggest battle is fought between themselves and their own mind.

Running requires physical and mental endurance. This is especially true for long-distance runners. Once separated from the pack, marathon or ultra-runners are alone with their thoughts for hours on end. But runners of all distances and levels, from novice upwards, can benefit from training the mind.

The techniques in this chapter are inspired by yogic concentration exercises and adapted to suit the runner. They will forge a self-reliant, positive and focused mindset: a serious ally in training or competition.

WHAT ARE YOU THINKING?

Elite level runners, from 100 metre sprinters through to ultra marathoners appreciate the power of the mind and the impact it has on performance. If two runners are equally matched in terms of physical fitness it can mean the difference between winning and loosing. They dedicate time to forging a mindset that is positive and 'in the moment' leaving no room for self-doubt. So how can state of mind alter running performance? Lets compare the 'trained' and 'untrained' mind of a runner.

The untrained mind

The untrained mind can be anxious, scattered and prone to negative thoughts. It spends a large amount of time mulling over the past and worrying about the future, questioning the capabilities of the physical body – a real liability for a long-distance runner.

1 BATTLING GREMLINS

Left to its own devices the mind is apt to randomly jump from one thought to another like a naughty primate – a state Buddhists call 'monkey mind'. These unpredictable thought patterns are both distracting and a liability for runners if those thoughts turn negative. These mental 'gremlins' might say 'you should have trained more' or 'you won't make it', undermining training and chipping away at confidence.

2 THE WANDERING MIND

Have you ever completed a run on automatic pilot without giving your body a second thought? Your heart is pumping, your legs pounding and arms swinging, but your mind is so busy mulling over work, bills or food shopping it doesn't register your body. You only reconnect to the physical when something hurts like that toenail rubbing or calf niggling.

3 REGRETTING AND ANTICIPATING

It's common to spend most of a race either analysing the past ('that was a poor start') or worrying about the future ('I'll never make 10 more miles'). This can easily trigger a negative downward spiral of despair and frustration. Yoga, and other Eastern disciplines, teach that dwelling on the past or the future causes suffering because we are either fretting over

something that cannot be changed or is total fantasy (note the wise quote: 'worrying is like praying for bad things to happen'). On a purely physical level this mental anxiety often manifests itself as muscular tension, usually in your jaw or shoulders. This affects running form and drains energy. The only moment you can influence is now, hence the emphasis in this chapter on anchoring the mind to the present.

The trained mind

The ideal running mindset is calm, focused, positive and anchored firmly in the present moment. It supports and motivates the body, so the runner operates as a single, strong mind/body unit. The trained mind can shut out distractions, either in the form of other runners or physical discomfort, and maintain unwavering focus for long periods – a real asset for a long-distance runner.

❛ *What separates good from almost-good runners is an ability to concentrate for an entire race.* ❜

Kara Goucher, US long-distance runner,
Runner's World magazine, May 2013

1 CONCENTRATING THE MIND

The trained mind is focused. Concentration is a key component of 'the zone', that state of pure 'flow' experienced by some runners, but remaining frustratingly elusive for others. Concentration is the skill of channelling your mind's scattered thoughts into one single direction through the use of techniques like mantra repetition, visualisation or breath-watching – all of which we will explore later in this chapter. This allows you to shed any irrelevant or negative thoughts and to focus purely on your running goal.

2 THINKING POSITIVE

A positive mindset is often what separates good athletes from great ones (note Muhammad Ali's uncompromising statement: 'I am the greatest!'). This self-belief will continue to propel your body long after a weaker mindset has given up. A carefully chosen mantra or longer affirmation hammers home the point and can even be repeated to synchronise with breathing and footfall. Steal one off a running legend or construct your own and repeat, repeat, repeat…

3 UNITING BODY AND MIND

Blocking out pain or using external distractions (counting lampposts or listening to music) are useful ways of soldiering on in a tough run or race, but they are essentially temporary. It's like the Buddhist saying: 'Wherever you go, there you are'. Once the music is turned off the mental gremlins or aches and pains resurface. In yoga, connecting mind and body (its ultimate aim) begins with simple breath awareness. Breathing is the link between the mental and physical. In this chapter and the next one you will learn how to become 'breath aware' while running. Then spread this awareness to the entire body via the running mindfully technique.

THINK POSITIVE

What are mantras?

'Mantra' means 'mind instrument' in Sanskrit and is a word or snappy phrase silently or audibly repeated over and over to jolt your mind into a certain state. They can be motivational or calming and are resolutely positive. Runners either use mantras as a pre-race confidence booster to tackle nerves and instil a feeling that they deserve to be there ('I'm strong and I'm ready'), or chant them mid-race to drown out pain or exhaustion ('I run fast, I run strong, I can run all day long'). Remember: 'The body achieves what the mind believes'.

Mantras must be:

1 **Personal:** Pick a word or phrase that boosts your weakest area. If you suffer from tension, chant 'relax and flow' and feel those shoulders drop. For improved posture say: 'form first, speed will follow'.

2 **Present:** Use 'I am' to draw yourself into the here and now. Yoga teaches that analysing the past and fretting about the future creates physical and mental stress. So forget your perceived 'poor' start and stop worrying if you can gain time.

3 **Positive:** Mantras are never negative. Embed upbeat instructions like 'I Can And I Am' to re-boot a flagging body.

4 **Active:** If you are tiring, say: 'run fast 'or 'run strong' to pick up the pace. It's the motivational equivalent of having a coach yelling in your ear. Other action words are: 'Power', 'Sprint', 'Go', or 'Speed'.

MANTRAS AND RUNNING RHYTHM

In the absence of motivational music on race day a longer mantra synchronised with your footfall will maintain running pace. Try: 'Form first and then the speed will follow' or 'Feet fast, legs strong, I can do this all day long'. The rhythm of the words should match your stride and breathing to encourage a feeling of flow with the mind and body working as one unit. Experiment with combinations of words using the suggestions on the next page to find a longer mantra, or affirmation, that fits nicely with your stride. Of course the aim is to get a motivational kick, but, if nothing else, timing a mantra with your footfall will pass the time and drown out any negative thoughts.

FAMOUS RUNNERS' MANTRAS

Struggling to dream up your own mantra?
Gain inspiration from the mantras of elite
runners and triathletes:

❝ Never, ever give up. ❞

Chrissie Wellington, World Ironman Champion

❝ Define yourself. ❞

Deena Kastor, American long-distance runner

❝ Be the best you can be each day. ❞

Paula Radcliffe, marathon world record holder

❝ Be water.❞ (from the Bruce Lee mantra).

Bolota Asmerom, American middle-distance runner

VISUALISATION

Many top athletes 'see' a race unfold in the mind's eye before the real event, as a way of calming nerves, gaining control and willing a desired outcome. Others use mental imagery mid-event to kick-start a flagging body by imagining themselves as an invincible machine or graceful tiger. Home-based and 'on-run' visualisations are both valid ways of using mental power to reinforce physical effort.

Visualisation benefits

In this internal home movie you dictate the action before it unfolds. The main benefit of practising this mental imagery is – in essence – confidence. Runners use it to:

1 Rehearse a race route so there are no surprises (see visualisation 1 below).

2 See themselves tackling the course with ease (see visualisation 2, page 175).

3 Boost the enjoyment of training (see visualisation 3, page 167).

4 Anchor their focus in the present moment (see visualisation 4, page 177).

5 Increase speed, power or agility (see visualisation 5, page 177).

How to visualise

1 **Find a quiet place:** either at home or sitting in the car, where you won't be disturbed or feel rushed.

2 **Get comfortable:** Sit with a straight back or lie down with your legs bent, feet on the floor.

3 **Breathe deeply:** Close your eyes and take five counting breaths, inhaling for three seconds and exhaling for four.

4 **Start small:** Don't conjure up an entire course or race in your first session. Hold an image in your head for just 30 seconds and gradually build up.

5 **Start static:** Sometimes it's easier to picture a static scene. If you are struggling to keep a movie rolling in your head try picturing a favourite beach or mountain top.

6 **Involve all your senses:** Don't just look but hear, listen and feel as well. For example, listen to the soft thud of your feet touching the ground and hear the swish of your rain resistant running top. Feel the wind or sun on your face.

7 **Think positive:** Visualisations can only be positive. The second a negative thought pops up, re-start the movie on your terms.

8 **Know your running:** Imagery will work best when you have attained a certain level of physical fitness and running skill. This is because you understand instinctively how it feels to run well and can replicate that in a virtual way.

Pre-run visualisations

VISUALISATION 1: THE DUMMY RUN

Use visual imagery as a practical tool to check you are 100 per cent prepared for the 'what-ifs' on race day. For example, picture yourself eating a nutritious, fuelling breakfast and feeling full of energy. See yourself packing your bag and know you haven't forgotten anything. Visualise calmly arriving, parking and registering with time to spare. How will you cope with blisters or a sudden change in weather in the form of hot sun or a rainstorm? Where will you refuel and hydrate? Familiarise yourself with the twists and turns of the course. Running through possible scenarios will boost confidence and ease race nerves leaving you free to enjoy the day knowing you are ready.

VISUALISATION 2: THE PERFECT RACE

Your body is primed and ready; is your mind? The perfect race lets you run the course as you would ideally love to. Remember: the unconscious mind doesn't differentiate between a real experience and an imagined one. So re-run the perfect race until it becomes ingrained in your mind. Start by seeing sections of the day in the mind's eye, gradually extending the length of your visualisation over time, but don't compromise on detail: the more vivid the better. For example, picture yourself at the start line. See the bright colours of your clothes, feel your feet cushioned in your trainers or the cool water bottle in your hand. What kind of emotions do you have: nerves, adrenaline or excitement? Hear the sounds of the race: competitors chatting or pacing back and forth in anticipation.

Move through the race visualising the following:

- running with good form
- hearing the crowds cheering
- tackling hills effortlessly
- feeling strong at the halfway mark
- surging to the finish line.

VISUALISATION 3: THE PERFECT RUN

The perfect run is designed to enhance the pure pleasure of running. Choose a familiar training route, the more picturesque the better. For example, imagine a forest trail or lakeside track. Since everything is 'perfect' see yourself running tall with effortless ease. Your shoulders are relaxed, arms swinging, and stride is smooth and light. There's no strain. The sun is warming your face and you feel a soft breeze on your skin. Everything is peaceful and calm. You can hear the sound of your breathing as smooth and fluid – moving in, moving out – in a calm, regular rhythm. Settle into a steady pace and soak up your surroundings, noticing the dustiness of the track or bright blueness of the sky. As you near the end of the run slow down and walk a little. Reward yourself with a long cool drink of water.

On-run visualisations

VISUALISATION 4:
THE RUNNING COMMENTARY

In the running commentary you are the star throughout the duration of a race or run. A cameraman tracks your progress, either filming alongside on the back of a bike, or from above, in a helicopter. The soundtrack is the channel's running commentary on you: your position in the race, energy levels, form or racing tactics. The beauty of this visualisation is that it allows the runner to maintain concentration throughout the length of a race or run and forces them to assess their performance. This process of continual monitoring prevents your mind wandering. It's also pretty motivational; it's hard to let the pace slow if you know you're being watched.

VISUALISATION 5:
CHEETAHS, PANTHERS AND WOLVES

Re-route your mind away from pain by imagining yourself as a strong, agile, fast animal. Select the animal you most identify with and then conjure it up when energy levels are flagging and you need a surge of power to accelerate or sprint uphill. Alternatively try to adopt other characteristics of the animal aside from its power and speed, such as the way it runs gracefully or quietly on its pads, undetected by runners in front. I know a runner who has a heavy heel strike and started using this 'feet as tiger paws' visualisation to land more softly and lightly. If it works, use it!

Real runner's visualisations

- 'A wire – one end attached to my forehead and the other a mile or so down the road attached to a winch, pulling me along.'
- 'In the last five miles of a marathon I visualise the route of an easy five mile run I have done countless times before.'
- 'I picture a magic carpet floating alongside myself that I can use just to take the weight off my feet. I don't use it for the whole race (that would be cheating).'
- 'I pretend there is fire or broken glass on the ground so my feet have as little contact with the ground as possible. This creates a lighter and faster step.'
- 'I imagine myself as a steam locomotive and the furnace is being stoked by Mars Bars.'

YOGA AND THE ZONE

' My sharpest and possibly most memorable experience of being in the 'zone' was during the World Cross Country Championships in Ostend in 2001, where I won the senior long race for the first time. That day, I felt surreally cool and in control. It was almost as though I knew what would happen before it did. A calm voice in my head seemed to tell me exactly what moves to make and when. I just knew I would win that race. '

Paula Radcliffe, *How to Run*, Simon & Schuster, 2011

The term 'zone' (or 'flow') was used by the researchers Susan A. Jackson and Mihaly Csikszentmihalyi in their book *Flow in Sports* (Human Kinetics, 1999) to describe a state where the athlete is 100 per cent absorbed in the task at hand. Athletes report varying sensations of total confidence, invincibility and even of time distortion, where actions appear to take place in dream-like slow motion.

Former sprinter Mark Richardson experienced the zone while competing in a 4 × 400 m relay in 1996 and described it using words like 'effortless' and 'floating'.

' Every muscle, every fibre, every sinew is working in complete harmony and the end product is that you run fantastically well. '

Mark Richardson, British 400 m sprinter, *Mind Games*, Grout and Perrin, Capstone Publishing, 2004

According to Csikszentmihalyi, there are nine characteristics of the zone. One is that 'action and awareness merge' to create a feeling of mind/body union. So rather than battling against a doubting, negative mind the athlete is operating as a single unit. Radcliffe was probably not thinking that much at all in Ostend in 2001, and obviously had no feelings of arousal or anxiety, whereas Richardson talked of 'seeing clearly' in his flow-like state. The minds of both athletes were uncluttered by doubt or irrelevant thoughts.

Concentration: The 'critical component'

Of all the zone characteristics, one dominates: concentration. The ability to exclude irrelevant thoughts from consciousness and focus utterly and completely on the race, game or match, is central to experiencing the zone in sport. It is from this focused state, for example, that your mind seems calmer and more in control and at one with your body.

WHAT IS CONCENTRATION?

What is concentration and how can you improve it? Here is a water-based analogy: imagine the everyday mental state as a bit like rainfall; thoughts just appear and land randomly without any pattern. However, concentrate and you channel this water into a stream or river so it is moving forcefully in one single direction. Concert pianists, artists and elite-level athletes all demonstrate high levels of concentration, displaying this ability to focus irrespective of what is occurring around them.

YOGA AND FLOW

Concentration, or 'dharana' in Sanskrit, is just one element of yoga's overall aim to 'settle the mind into silence' (from *The Yoga Sutras*, Patanjali, third century BC). Settling the mind is a tall order for the average runner! The feeling of uninterrupted flow enjoyed by some lucky athletes is what serious yoga students spend decades striving to achieve, but Csikszentmihalyi points out the similarities between the two:

‘ The similarities between yoga and flow are extremely strong; in fact it makes sense to think of yoga as a very thoroughly planned flow activity. Both are trying to achieve a joyous, self-forgetful involvement through concentration, which in turn is made possible by a discipline of the body… it is not unreasonable to regard yoga as one of the oldest and most systematic methods of producing the flow experience. ’

Mihaly Csikszentmihalyi, *Flow*
(Harper & Row, 1992)

In yoga, dharana translates as 'one-pointedness' or 'steadiness of mind', and means holding or fixing the attention steadily on an object, sound or thought. It is stage six of the eight stages of yoga. The first two stages concern the rules for living (truthfulness, non-attachment, contentment). The following stages include the physical postures, breathing exercises, concentration, and meditation and enlightenment.

Any good yoga class will give a tiny taster of a 'settled mind' even if you simply walk out thinking a little calmer and clearer than when you walked in. In reality yoga's stages are intertwined. For example, the physical postures release mental, as well as physical stress and concentration is required to hold Tree balance. So while enlightenment is just not realistic for your average runner, improved concentration is an achievable goal.

Simple concentration techniques

1 PHYSICAL: TREE BALANCE

All yoga postures build concentration, but the balances really focus the mind. To try tree, spread the toes and shift the weight onto the left foot. Anchor the gaze to a point on the floor or wall ahead. Slowly lift the right foot, turn the knee out and press the foot into the ankle or thigh of the standing leg. Bring the palms together at the chest in a prayer position. Remain here for five to ten breaths.

2 VISUAL: OBJECT VISUALISATION

If you are new to visualising, this simple technique is a good place to start. Place an object – such as an apple – in your palm and study it closely. The more detail you can absorb the better: colour, shape, texture or smell. Take time to notice it in fine detail. Now close your eyes and recreate the apple in your mind's eye. See how long you can hold the image before it fades.

Creating your own 'flow'

The exact nature of the zone remains a mystery and many zone experiences are spontaneous events that seem to take runners by surprise. In this sense they cannot will themselves into the zone, or all athletes would be in a constant state of peak performance.

There are many ways, though, of re-creating elements of 'flow' albeit on a smaller scale. It is entirely possible to run with less tension and a calmer, more focused mind. Many techniques to achieve this are outlined in this book and include:

- observing your breathing
- creating a rhythmic breathing pattern
- running with a comfortable, balanced posture
- relaxing your shoulders, arms and hands
- releasing physical tension through yoga postures
- repeating a mantra to focus your mind
- training your mind through seated meditation
- exploring a running meditation.

3 AURAL: MANTRA REPETITION

Mantra is a sound, syllable, word or group of words that are repeated to aid concentration. The choice of word or words is important as mantras can calm or motivate. Running mantras, such as those used earlier in this chapter, are mostly designed to energise. However, if you want to use mantra purely as a way of drowning out mental chatter and improving general concentration, then choose a simple one like 'peace'.

4 TACTILE: BREATH-WATCHING

Breath-watching is probably the most important concentration skill you can learn, and not just for running (see 'Running mindfully' at the end of this chapter for an 'on-run' variation). It will clear your head in everyday stressful or complex situations when you can't think straight, and can be performed anywhere you can sit for a minute. Simply focus all your attention on your nostrils.

Observe your breath as it flows in and out without deliberately deepening or altering it. Every time your mind wanders draw it back to this tiny area and begin again.

RUNNING: A MOVING MEDITATION

You may have heard runners describe their sport as 'meditative'. But what do they mean? All runners know that a good run can help shed the worries and anxieties that have accumulated through the day. They end the run feeling happier and thinking clearer.

Other times, however, we remain stuck 'in our heads,' throughout the run, arriving back home to the front door on automatic pilot with no awareness of the physical body – we've missed the entire event. As we have seen, the mind can also dominate during races, especially in times of fatigue.

There are several methods of taming the mind while running, from the very simple – counting from one to ten – to running mindfully. Some are straightforward while others require practice and dedication just like physical training.

Linking home and running meditation

If you've never tried seated meditation or concentration exercises I recommend experimenting with it at home first, even preceded by a yoga relaxation or some deep breathing. This is why each running meditation is preceded by a seated version.

Home-based meditation lets you examine the workings of your mind without the distractions of traffic, rain or other runners. This will only serve to reinforce the power you have over your mind when running. Make sure you are not disturbed, and sit cross-legged, kneeling or on a chair, with a straight spine and eyes closed. Chapter 11 contains more home-based meditations.

Finally, experiment with running meditations on a familiar training run. The more you are acquainted with every rock or lamppost, the less you'll be thinking about where you are going. This leaves more time to focus on your mind.

Try the following linked home-based and running meditations

1–10 MEDITATION

This is a simple, but effective way of keeping your mind occupied, so it's ideal for those new to meditation. Just sit comfortably and count silently (or audibly if this is easier) from one to ten as follows:

• Inhale	'one'		• Exhale	'six'
• Exhale	'two'		• Inhale	'seven'
• Inhale	'three'		• Exhale	'eight'
• Exhale	'four'		• Inhale	'nine'
• Inhale	'five'		• Exhale	'ten'

If your mind wanders, begin again.

1–10 RUNNING

' When I count to 100 three times, it's a mile. It helps me focus on the moment and not think about how many miles I have to go. I concentrate on breathing and striding, and I go within myself. '

Paula Radcliffe, *The Oxford Handbook of Sport and Performance Psychology*, **Shane Murphy**, **Oxford University Press, 2012.**

Paula Radcliffe shares her trusty counting method, which is both a pacing mechanism and a concentration technique. Counting to 100, however, takes practice. If you feel your mind is likely to wander before you reach that number, try counting 1–10 and keep repeating. Choose a foot and count every time that foot touches the floor, or count 'one' for your right foot and a second 'one' for your left. If your mind wanders, begin again counting silently or say the numbers aloud.

1–10 in triathlon

If you are a triathlete (or duathlete) try using the 1–10 method in the swim and/or bike section to provide a simple mental theme that threads through the race, linking your two or three sports. In cycling count 'one' for the right foot, and a second 'one' for the left. This way you encourage an even pedal stroke on both sides, rather than only pushing down harder on the right or 'counting' side. In swimming try the same method, counting 'one' for each stroke to make both strokes more even. The 1–10 method in triathlon keeps your mind focused and also encourages a consistent pace throughout the race.

Breath-watching meditation

Like most meditations, breath watching doesn't ask you to 'empty your mind' (a meditation myth). Instead it anchors your attention onto your breath, which is portable, free and always there, unlike meditation recordings or teachers. Sit comfortably. Take a few slow deep breaths then deliberately let your breathing drop into a subtle, quiet pattern. Focus your attention on the space between your nostrils and start to notice the ebb and flow of your breath.

- Try not to alter your breathing by deliberately deepening it.
- Resist anticipating your next inhalation or exhalation.
- Notice the warmth or texture of your breath.

When your mind wanders, draw it back to this space between your nostrils and start observing again.

BREATH-WATCHING RUNNING

The running version of this meditation will be a lot less subtle. Firstly there is the environmental noise of traffic, wind or your feet hitting the ground. Secondly, the breathing will be harder and faster and probably through the mouth. This is fine. This technique is still about observation rather than deepening your breathing, or finding a 'correct' way to breathe. Hone in on the pace and rhythm of your breath. Listen to it – without judging the sound as good or bad.

Mindfulness meditation

This meditation is based on the Buddhist concept of 'mindfulness'. Being 'mindful' is to be constantly aware of sensations in the body without labelling them 'good' or 'bad'. In running terms this means a hamstring twinge is simply a hamstring twinge and does not trigger a flood of anxious thoughts about potential future injury. We lessen discomfort by not reacting emotionally to it.

Like the breath-watching meditation, this technique is based on observation. However, this time it incorporates the entire body. Sit comfortably. Begin by repeating the breath-watching technique. Then start to expand your awareness by noticing how your torso moves as you breathe in and out or feeling the pressure of your pelvis or legs on the floor. If discomfort arises in the form of an aching back, for example, notice this but don't get drawn into an emotional response. Monitor your body in a cool, detached way as if standing next to yourself with a clipboard and pen making clinical observations.

RUNNING MINDFULLY

Transport the technique to running by making similar regular body scans. This will both occupy your mind and also provide useful continual feedback as to your posture, pace or breathing. The last benefit of mindful running (and possibly the most useful during distance races) is how it stops you becoming anxious about niggles and discomfort. This takes practice! But diligent practice both at home and out running, will create a mind that is not easily swayed by the challenges that running throws at us.

Begin with your breathing by:
- observing the rhythm of your breathing
- listening to the sound of your breathing
- observing the sensation of your breath in your abdomen or chest.

Remember: there are no 'good' or 'bad' sounds or feelings. Your breathing is just where you anchor your attention. Every time it wanders, bring it back.

Now expand your awareness by conducting systematic full body scans. These scans can be performed randomly or at mile markers during a race, and begin and end with breath observation.

For example:
- Observe the rhythm, sound and sensation of your breathing.
- Observe your shoulders – are they tight or relaxed?
- Observe your arms – are they swinging freely or stiff?
- Observe your back – is it straight, slumped or leaning forwards?
- Observe your hips – are they tight or mobile?
- Observe your legs – does your stride feel free or restricted? Where?
- Observe your feet – are they landing heavily or softly? Can you hear them?
- Return to the rhythm, sound and sensation of your breath.

10

BREATH CONTROL

> **' I learnt the concept of Pranayama (literally, 'extension of the life force' breathing) which would help, not just my body, but my mind and emotions as well. '**
>
> Scott Jurek, *Eat and Run* (Bloomsbury, 2012)

Runners train their bodies and minds, so why not train their breathing? True, for many runners, respiration is as automatic as blinking or swallowing, and rarely considered until they are 'short of breath'. But yoga has many techniques to transform an automatic function into a performance tool, whether you want to breathe more efficiently, maintain pace or calm pre-race nerves.

Many of these techniques work to modulate the depth and frequency of breathing. Quick gulps are gradually replaced by fewer and slower abdominal, or diaphragmatic breaths. This is especially useful for novice runners who gasp ineffectually for air until fitness levels improve, but it can make breathing while running less laboured and more comfortable for runners of all levels.

BREATH TRAINING FOR RUNNERS

The breathing techniques in this chapter have their roots in yoga's ancient discipline of Pranayama. The name translates variously as the 'expansion or extension of *prana*' with *prana* being energy or 'life force' (a concept similar to Chinese chi). Even if you are sceptical about the idea of *prana*, the simple concept that by controlling the breathing you begin to manage the mind is a useful one for runners. Being an endurance sport, running success depends partly on strength of mind. Monitoring the breathing is one straightforward way of focusing the mind, thereby not allowing it to wander on to negative thoughts. Pranayama techniques might deliberately extend the inhalation and exhalation, or experiment with ratios (see breath/stride ratios, page 197). Or they may serve a calming purpose by levelling a turbulent mind.

Remember: introduce any new breathing techniques gradually, taking account of cardiovascular or respiratory problems.

The benefits of breath control for runners

STAYING PHYSICALLY RELAXED

Not only is grabbing quick breaths, or panting, an ineffective way to transport oxygen to the leg muscles, it also makes us tense, triggering a range of sympathetic nervous responses, from locked shoulders to clenched jaws.

Conscious, deep breathing is an important part of the process of keeping the body fluid and relaxed during running, as explored in Chapter 3. The other elements of reducing stress are mental training methods, physical stretching and relaxation.

KEEPING MENTALLY CALM AND FOCUSED

The effect of panting on the runner is not just physical; erratic breathing patterns can create an anxious, or negative mindset, a hindrance in a race when adrenaline levels are already soaring. Bring your breathing under control and this mental tension will ease, leading to more relaxed physical form.

RUNNING IN COMFORT

Of most interest to runners is probably the effect that breathing slowly and deeply will have on comfort levels. The diaphragm is a muscle built for endurance due to its high percentage of slow twitch fibres. Breathing more with the diaphragm uses a lot less energy than breathing higher in the upper chest and throat as we do when panting. These fast-twitch, secondary respiratory muscles in the upper chest and neck, are just not designed to be used for long periods of time and fatigue quickly.

OPTIMISING LUNG CAPACITY

It should be noted that no amount of breath training will increase the size of the lungs (a shame for runners!). However, we can optimise our existing capacity. The average resting person uses just 10–15 per cent of their lungs to breathe. Many Pranayama techniques teach us to take a fuller, or more complete inhalation, especially the three-part breath technique.

Choosing your level of breath control

'Training' your breath can mean something as simple as tuning into the rhythm of your breathing to maintain pace. There are many reasons to explore breath training or control.

Here are a few:

- To maintain a consistent pace.
- To enhance lung capacity.
- To anchor a wandering mind during long runs or races.
- To distract your mind from physical exhaustion.
- To alleviate boredom during marathon or ultra events.
- To help create a physically relaxed and fluid running stride.
- To investigate the idea of nasal breathing and running.

Follow the steps to increased breathing control in this sequence:

1 Stretching the torso.
2 Breath awareness.
3 Where do you breathe?
4 Abdominal breathing.
5 Optimising lung capacity.
6 Counting breaths.
7 Exhaling longer.

Breathing: posture and core

Running form greatly affects our ability to breathe properly. Poor posture manifesting as a curved spine, rounded shoulders or a protruding head collapses your chest making it harder for your lungs to inflate and ribcage to expand. Rocking the torso, or swinging the arms from side to side places additional demands on breathing as the upper and lower halves of the body counter-rotate. The breathing muscles also help control running posture and stabilise the core. Breath training will be more effective, therefore, once good posture and a strong core are established. See Chapter 2 and Chapter 7 for techniques on both.

After a few weeks of assimilating these basic breathing lessons at home explore some 'on-run' techniques.

HOME-BASED BREATHING TECHNIQUES

Step 1: Stretching the torso

Like all other muscles those wrapping around the ribcage benefit from a good stretch. Put simply; the more supple your torso, the deeper you are able to breathe as locked muscles cannot expand freely as your lungs inflate. These stretches have supplementary benefits. The side-bend provides a satisfying stretch in an area commonly tight in runners, while the backbend draws back your shoulders, improving posture. Forward-bending is also a simple way to wind down a busy mind. If sitting cross-legged is uncomfortable, kneel or stand.

Stay for five to ten breaths in each stretch.

Side: Release your right fingertips to the floor and side-bend to the right, sweeping the left arm up and over. Then place your left palm on the left side of your ribcage and press gently. You might feel the muscles of your ribcage slowly expanding and contracting as you breathe. Switch sides.

Back: Interlace your fingers in front, palms facing you. Tuck your chin in to stretch the back of your neck and round your back so that you can feel your shoulder blades spreading apart.

Front: Draw your shoulders back and interlace your hands behind your back. Lift your breastbone and feel your chest and shoulders opening.

Step 2: Breath awareness

Breath awareness may sound like a 'miss-able' step in the journey to breath control, but it's a vital one. Many of us have never noticed how we breathe so need to just sit for a moment and observe the process. Close your eyes. Try not to deliberately 'deep breathe' so your respiration is natural, and breathe through your nose.

Notice the following:

- Is your breath smooth or jagged?
- Is it audible?
- Is the inhalation and exhalation equal?
- Is there a pause after the inhalation and exhalation?
- Is it difficult to breathe through your nose?

At this stage there are no 'good' or 'bad' ways to breathe. This is just a simple way to start to tune into your breathing before moving on to more technical breathing exercises. Breath awareness is also a straightforward way to start a yoga practice, relax or prepare for meditation. I begin teaching every yoga class with breath awareness. On a practical front it may highlight issues such as difficulty with nasal breathing that will be useful to know later on. This simple process of observation can also be repeated in the first few minutes of a run.

Step 3: Where do you breathe?

The old-fashioned idea of breathing deeply was to take a quick, sharp breath that inflated the chest. We now know that, both in everyday life and in running, the ideal way to breathe is roughly 80 per cent with the diaphragm, the primary respiratory muscle. The secondary respiratory muscles in the neck and upper chest, like the sternocleidomastoid and the trapezius, should take up the remaining 20 per cent of the task.

This 80/20 ratio is one to aim for while running, but breathing like this will also keep you cool and calm in the face of life's general stresses. Notice that when you are faced with a stressful situation or emergency your breathing feels higher in your chest. When we are anxious the ratio is more likely to be 50/50, accompanied by raised shoulders, a tightness between your shoulder blades, and even around your neck and jaw.

Types of breathing

- Upper chest: Also called 'clavicular' breathing in yoga. Someone breathing primarily using the secondary respiratory muscles tends to take short, sharp, shallow breaths and might feel tension in the neck, shoulders, between the shoulder blades and even around the jaw.
- Chest: We are taught that taking a deep breath means inflating the chest, but chest breathing isn't the most natural or efficient or sustainable way to breathe and is likely to trigger the body's 'fight or flight' stress response.
- Abdominal: Fluid, steady and sustainable; breathe more from the abdominal region and you are shifting more of the breathing role to your primary respiratory muscles: your diaphragm and abdominal muscles.

Lie down with your legs bent and feet on the floor, hip-distance apart. Simply place one palm on your abdomen and one palm on your chest. Close your eyes. Notice which hand moves as you breathe. Most people will notice movement in both the abdomen and chest, but one may predominate. Ideally you are working towards a completely still upper hand with your lower hand visibly rising and falling on each inhalation and exhalation.

The diaphragm: made for endurance

The diaphragm, a large dome-shaped muscle that sits in the chest like a parachute, comprises 80 per cent slow-twitch fibres making it ideal for endurance sports. Slow twitch fibres are more efficient at using oxygen to liberate energy over a long period of time. It requires a lot less energy to breathe primarily using the diaphragm than the delicate respiratory muscles (inspiratory intercostals, sternomastoids and scalenes) around the neck, upper back and upper chest. This is because these secondary muscles fire quickly but tire easily. Pain or discomfort around this upper chest and neck area is not uncommon among runners signaling that these secondary or accessory muscles are doing too much. These muscles are also less efficient at bringing about changes in lung volume meaning that they must work relatively harder than the diaphragm to generate a given breath volume.

Step 4: Abdominal breathing

This simple technique shifts the breathing more into the abdominal region and thereby increases the role of the diaphragm. Once mastered, experiment with abdominal breathing standing, then running, but be aware that due to its stabilising role the belly won't inflate as much as it does when practising in a relaxed supine position.

Lie down with your legs bent and feet on the floor, hip-distance apart. Place both palms on your abdomen so that your fingertips touch. Close your eyes. As you breathe in allow your belly to rise so your fingertips move slightly apart. As you breathe out let your belly deflate and your fingertips reconnect. Breathe only through your nose. Repeat five times.

THE RESISTANCE BAND TECHNIQUE

This Yoga Sports Science® technique uses an elastic resistance band wrapped around the torso to encourage diaphragmatic breathing. The technique has the added benefit of strengthening the inspiratory respiratory muscles. Choose a wide band and wrap it tightly around the widest part of your ribcage. The band should lie smooth and flat to your body. Sit tall and close your eyes. Slowly breathe in expanding your ribcage outwards into the band until you feel the resistance. Exhale and sense a slight slacking of the band.

Note: these are not big movements. Taking a few deep breaths before applying the band may help if you are finding it hard to focus on the subtle nature of the technique. Take five to ten slow breaths noting if the movement increases a little on each inhalation. If you don't own a resistance band use the palms of your hands, pressed against your ribs as a substitute.

Step 5: Optimising lung capacity

We can't make our lungs bigger, but we can optimise our existing capacity. This exercise focuses on taking a more complete inhalation.

Lie down with your legs bent and feet on the floor, hip-distance apart.

1 Repeat the abdominal breathing technique with your palms on your belly. Take four breaths.

2 Slide your hands up and out to the sides of your rib cage. Press lightly so you can feel your ribs. Focus on inhaling into your palms. Notice how your ribcage expands both outwards and sideways into your hands as you breathe in. Take four breaths.

3 Rest your fingertips on your collar bones and imagine you can breathe into this upper section of your chest. Take four breaths.

4 Link all three techniques. Split the inhalation into three. Breathe the first third into your abdomen, roll the second third into your chest and inhale the final third into your upper chest.

Slowly release the exhalation through your nose and begin again.

Step 6: Counting breaths

Counting your breath is a very simple way to improve breath awareness and paves the way for experimenting with breath/stride ratios during running. Remain lying. Close your eyes. Breathe in through your nose for a count of three seconds and breathe out for a count of three. If this is a comfortable count then stay with it, or extend the count to four. Repeat five times. This technique can also be performed sitting or standing.

Step 7: Exhaling longer

A simple trick to practise at home while doing simple deep breathing exercises such as abdominal breathing and later transfer to running is to exhale longer. Why? Because exhaling longer:

- expels more carbon dioxide
- triggers a deeper inhalation, thereby kick-starting a deeper, slower breathing pattern
- aids recovery when you abruptly run out of breath during a hill ascent or sprint and literally feel there's no air left in your lungs
- helps avoid the instinct to pant rapidly through your mouth – an inefficient method of transferring oxygen to the muscles
- calms your mind, keeping thinking clear and focused.

Sit or lie down with your legs bent and feet hip-distance apart. Take a deep abdominal breath or roll the inhalation from abdomen to your upper chest (see step 4 opposite). Now purse your lips and blow out the exhalation in a slow, controlled manner. Continue breathing out until you feel your lungs empty. Notice how much slower and deeper the next in-breath is. Repeat five times. Resume normal breathing, but take a second to observe the relaxing effect.

ON RUN BREATHING TECHNIQUES

Once you have created a degree of 'on mat' breathing awareness and control, it's time to begin experimenting while running. The degree to which you explore 'on-run' breathing techniques will depend on your fitness levels.

NOVICE RUNNERS

Those new to running may still be struggling to find a comfort level with breathing as the body adapts, often feeling 'out of breath'. Therefore, simple breath awareness is sufficient at this stage. Notice if you are gasping for breath or panting and, if so, slow the pace, or intersperse periods of running with walking, until respiration becomes more comfortable. Focus on relaxing your shoulders and breathing more from your abdomen.

EXPERIENCED RUNNERS

Experienced runners have the freedom to play with run/breath ratios, perhaps by extending the exhalation, or may begin to think about incorporating elements of nasal breathing into their running.

Observing the breath

The best way to start connecting with your breathing is to take a few moments to observe it, just as you did on the mat. This is a useful tuning in process to assess practical physical factors, such as a blocked nose, which will slightly impair breathing, or tiredness levels. For example, is your breathing a bit laboured or smooth and easy? Listening to your breathing is also the first stage of mentally focusing on the run. By listening to the sound, or feeling the movement of your breathing you can shut out irrelevant or negative thoughts and start to run more 'mindfully' (see chapter 9).

The pros and cons of music

The motivational boost that music provides in training is undisputed. Studies show music reduces a runner's perception of how hard he is training by around 10 per cent. Aside from providing an injection of energy, music also elevates your mood, even promoting that flow-like state that many runners desire. However, if you are absorbed in music, you can't hear yourself breathing. In yoga, the breath is the mind/body link. Music breaks this link, shutting the head off from the rest of the body. It drowns out the breathing rhythm and also the sound of the foot strike; two useful performance indicators. Music can also be a bit of a mental crutch for some runners; as long as it's playing there's no need to tackle those disruptive thoughts that can undermine training or racing. A compromise would be to train with music, but once a week go without (and ditch pacing gadgets like running watches) and tune into your breathing.

Breath/stride ratios

A simple way to bring breath awareness into running is to synchronise breathing with running cadence or stride. You may well do this automatically, or have your own synchronised system. If not, consider the additional benefits to be gained by entraining breath and footfall. According to Alison McConnell, Professor of Applied Physiology at Brunel University, UK, synchronising breath and cadence 'minimises the competition between the stabilising and breathing functions of the breathing muscles'. McConnell writes in her book *Breathe Strong, Perform Better* (Human Kinetics, 2001) that without this system of entrainment, the respiratory movements of the diaphragm are impeded by the abdominal viscera (stomach, gut, liver), which rise and fall as you run. By breathing in time with stride frequency a runner can ensure that the diaphragm is 'assisted by the downward movement of the viscera'.

Breath/stride ratios work as follows:

First choose a 'counting' foot. Now link that foot strike with your breathing by beginning to inhale as it touches the ground. If you are using a relaxed 3:3 breathing ratio (see over the page) you will inhale over three foot strikes and then exhale over the following three. Reach a hill, however, and the ratio will need to be shortened to a 2:2 to get sufficient oxygen to those quads. On the next page are some suggestions for ratios according to speed and terrain, but experiment to see what works for you.

Stitches and breathing rhythm

Side stitches are thought to be caused either by diaphragmatic cramp or diaphragmatic 'ischaemia', or insufficient blood flow for the metabolic demand. Shallow, rapid breathing can bring on a stitch, so aim to maintain a 3:3 breathing ratio as a preventative measure. While this is not a scientifically proven remedy for stitches, some runners report finding it helps to change their breath/stride pattern. For example, if you are inhaling as your right foot strikes, switch to your left and start breathing in every time this foot hits the ground.

WARM-UP/EASY RATIO

A 3:3 ratio is a good ratio for a warm-up or relaxed pace. As your right foot hits the ground begin to breathe in and continue to inhale for two more right foot strikes. Then slowly release the exhalation in the same way – during three foot-strikes of your right foot.

RACE PACE AND HILLS

As you pick up your pace try a 2:2 ratio; inhaling as your right foot hits the ground twice and repeating the process as you breathe out. This ratio should work on hill ascents, providing the hill is not too steep.

SPRINTING

Again, try a 2:2 ratio. A 1:1 is too fast to breathe, because it does not allow sufficient time for a gaseous exchange to occur and may result in panting and light-headedness.

The foot strike question

There has been some research in recent years concerning the foot strike during rhythmic breathing. We know that when the foot hits the ground an impact of two to three times the body weight is transferred through the body. According to Budd Coates, the *Runner's World* coach, this stress is greatest when the foot strikes the ground at the beginning of an exhalation. The theory is that when a runner exhales the diaphragm and associated muscles relax, destabilising the core, which makes him or her vulnerable to injury. The solution is to alternate the foot that strikes as you start to breathe in so that one foot (and side of the body) doesn't always take the impact of exhaling. According to Coates, the process of alternating involves breathing in for a count of three and exhaling for two. This is quite a long inhalation in comparison with the yogic approach of an equal inhale/exhale or a longer exhale. The answer is: experiment! Personally, I find a longer exhale lets my shoulders drop and relax, and encourages a deeper overall rhythm, but I am now also ensuring that I periodically shift sides so I'm not always hitting the ground on the start of the out-breath with the same foot.

Introducing longer exhalations

The natural next step is to play with lengthening the exhalation. A longer exhale expels more CO_2 and helps create a feeling of relaxed control. When your mind is calm, your body will stay free of tension. Begin experimenting with extending your out-breath during a training run. Ensure you are running an easy pace on flat terrain, and play with making your exhalation just one count longer – a 2:3 or 3:4.

HILL RECOVERY TECHNIQUE

To recover quickly from a steep hill run while everyone around you is doubled up or gasping for air, try slowing down your breathing by pursing your lips and blowing your exhalation out slowly through your mouth (visualise a drinking straw). This long, controlled exhalation forces your body to suck in a slower inhalation, thereby kick-starting a slower overall breathing pattern. Your breathing will return to normal much faster, leaving you to continue with your run without stopping. If you are forced to stop don't collapse forwards, which compresses your abdomen, but tip to 90° by placing your hands on your knees. Or remain standing and take your hands behind your head to allow space for your lungs to fully inflate.

On-run nasal breathing

NASAL BREATHING AND YOGA
Nasal breathing is the default method of respiration when practising yoga. This is partly because breathing through the nose allows the air to be warmed and moistened before it reaches the lung tissue. It is also cleaned as it swirls through long passageways of nasal hair and mucus that trap dust, bacteria or tiny particles.

It is also easier to control and manipulate air that is passing through your nose simply because it takes longer to inflate your lungs. Take a deep breath with your mouth wide open noting the time this takes. Now repeat the experiment, but taking a deep nasal breath. It takes longer to suck the air through those tiny passages.

This means that the breathing rhythm remains slow and deep throughout the physical yoga practice – a calm constant, even during the most strenuous postures.

CAN RUNNER'S BREATHE NASALLY?
The nagging question remains: can these benefits of nasal breathing be transferred to running? The argument for nasal breathing was voiced most predominantly by John Douillard in his book *Body, Mind and Spirit*, first published in 1994 and which regularly re-surfaces in articles and running website chat rooms. The ultra-running specialist Scott Jurek is one of the most high-profile runners to convert. Some coaches, however, remain adamant that oral breathing is the quickest and most effective way to transfer oxygen to muscles.

AN ORAL/NASAL COMBINATION
While most runners unconsciously breathe through both mouth and nose, some settle on a combination. The most common approach is to breathe in through the nose and out through the mouth. This system allows some of the calming side effects of nasal breathing without the full conversion. As with all breathing techniques, it is important to introduce it gradually. Experiment with the technique initially during your warm-up jog, and in the last

> **One of the most important things you can do as an ultra-runner is to breathe abdominally, and a good way to learn that skill is to practise breathing nasally … Once you've mastered that, try nasal breathing (in and out through the nose) while you're running easy routes. For more difficult runs, like hills, or tempo workouts, breathe in through the nose, then exhale forcefully through the mouth (akin to what yoga practitioners call 'breath of fire').**
>
> **Eventually you should be able to breathe through your nose for entire easy runs and to inhale nasally during the less strenuous sections of even 100-mile runs … Nasal breathing humidifies and cleans the air. As a bonus, it allows you to eat quickly and breathe at the same time, whether running easy or hard.**

Scott Jurek, *Eat and Run* (Bloomsbury, 2012)

few moments of the cool-down jog. The oral exhalation can also be controlled and narrowed by pursing your lips and blowing the air out through an imaginary large straw just like the exhaling longer technique. Over time narrow the air passage to further refine the flow of air.

FULL NASAL BREATHING

Adapting fully to nasal breathing is a big undertaking and a technique that should be introduced little by little over a long period of time. I would recommend asking a Yoga Sports Coach™ to guide you through the process from mat to run (to search the global network of coaches go to www. yogasportscience.com).

Why? Most of us rarely think about our breathing at all. This means we need to start at the beginning by cultivating an 'on mat' awareness of correct breathing technique without the multiple distractions of running. See the case study over the page to find out how nasal breathing improved fatigue levels and recovery for one marathoner. But first, read how Scott Jurek converted:

CASE STUDY: A MARATHON RUNNER AND NASAL BREATHING

Yoga Sports Coach™ Anthea Sweet helped 42-year-old marathon runner Bob Bevil adapt to nasal breathing over a nine-week period, and studied the effect on respiratory strength, levels of fatigue and rate of recovery.

Bevil had been running for fifteen years, completing five marathons (personal best: 4 hours 13 minutes, London, 2009) and approximately fifty half-marathons (personal best: 1 hour 50 minutes, Henley, 2005).

Although Bevil possessed a tough mental mindset for endurance running he described himself as a 'plodder' and expressed a desire to run for longer without tiring. He also suffered considerable post-run muscular pain and stiffness, both in training and racing.

Regarding breathing patterns, Bevil complained of shortness of breath while running. He was able to breathe nasally on the inhalation for two or three miles, before switching to oral breathing, at which point the breathing became 'disorganised' for the remainder of the run.

Sweet conducted a range of simple tests to establish vital capacity (the maximum amount of air expelled after a maximum inhalation) and VO$_2$ max (the maximum amount of oxygen in millilitres than the body can use in one minute, per kilogram of body weight).

The main test, however, was the treadmill test (on the flat: 5.5 km/hour for 5 minutes, 8.8 km/hour for 2 minutes, finally setting the speed at 11.2 km/hour). This test was designed to indicate at what point the subject needed to stop nasal breathing and open his mouth to breathe. He began oral breathing after 1 minute 10 seconds.

Sweet introduced nasal breathing gradually over a nine-week period, at the end of which Bevil had scheduled his next half-marathon in Reading. The process of incorporating nasal breathing included alternate nostril breathing (see rest and recovery in the next chapter, page 212) to establish any nasal blockages, and ratio breathing (see breath/stride ratios, page 197) to extend the exhalation and pace the breath.

Alongside the 'on-mat' breathing and stretching work, the runner recorded levels of fatigue and rated his breathing experience after each run. Most importantly, he recorded how far into the run he opened his mouth for 'emergency' or oral breathing.

At the end of the nine-week period Bevil was breathing nasally, switching to oral breathing only for inclines and sprinting. Sweet conducted the same series of tests. In the main treadmill test Bevil was still comfortably breathing nasally at 15 minutes (at which point Sweet turned off the stopwatch), in comparison with 1 minute 10 seconds pre-intervention. Bevil claimed he could have 'run like that for another hour'. He commented that he was beginning to breathe 'almost naturally' through the nose, especially on in the inhalation.

The results from additional tests indicated an increased breathing capacity. For example, Bevil was able to exhale for 69 per cent longer in one of the vital capacity tests and his breathing rate at rest had decreased by over 8 per cent, suggesting the efficiency of each breath had increased.

His Reading half-marathon time was 1 hour 52 minutes, making it his third fastest half-marathon. He also beat his previous Reading personal best by approximately five minutes (or 4.6 per cent). A further interesting side effect of the nasal breathing experiment was a big reduction in muscle soreness following the event. Bevil reported feeling 'normal' aside from a slight tightness in the quadriceps. He also talked of feeling 'calmer' before the race and 'much more comfortable and relaxed' during it.

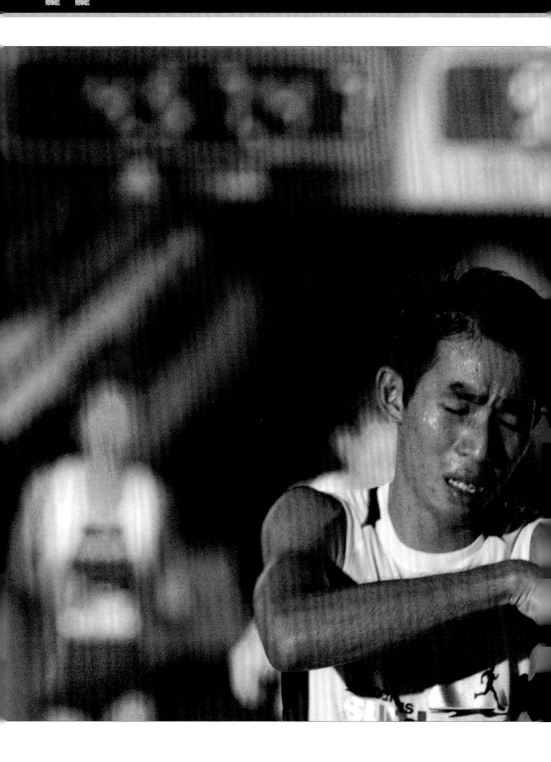

' Practising yoga is like pressing the 'reset' button for both body and mind. It eases tight muscles, reduces the fatigue of training and allows me to be ready to train hard again the next day. '

Duncan Haughey, chairman,

Elmbridge Road Runners, UK

The word 'recovery' simply means a day off pounding the streets for many runners. This chapter explores the concept of optimising this precious time off through a variety of techniques designed to let you return to running refreshed and recharged.

No-effort 'restorative' postures are held for longer to tease out muscular tension after days of training. Guided relaxations and breathing techniques engage the 'rest and restore' parasympathetic nervous system and simple meditations wind down a busy mind after a hard day's work. All these techniques prep the mind and body for the oldest and best recovery remedy of all: a good night's sleep.

RESTORATIVE POSTURES

Yoga's restorative postures are a treat for a tired runner. Held for up to five minutes they offer ample time for even the tightest muscles to lengthen. Performed statically, with the eyes closed, restorative postures are also very relaxing and prepare body and mind for further relaxation or deep sleep. The idea is not to push or strain, but to let the body slowly unravel. To facilitate this muscular release, restorative poses do require some care to set up, so have a pile of cushions handy to place under knees or behind the head for comfort. The following range of postures will move the spine through forward-bends, twists and side-bends ending in a position to freshen up tired legs.

Hold each posture for between one and five minutes.

TORTOISE

Tortoise stretches your back, neck, hips and adductors.

Tortoise is the ultimate relaxing forward-bend. Any posture that allows the head to hang down will have a soporific effect, so practise it if plagued by insomnia. There are no real rules – just round your back, let your head drop and curl into your shell – how deeply you fold in is up to you.

Sit and bring the soles of your feet together so your legs form a diamond shape. Hold on to your ankles and use that leverage to rock onto the front of your pelvis so your upper body tips forwards. Let your spine curve slowly and allow your head to drop. Either rest your palms on top of your lower legs or ankles, or go deeper, sliding your hands under your legs and holding your feet. Stay higher if there are any problems with your lower back.

RELAXED TWIST

Relaxed twist stretches your glutes, hips, torso, back and shoulders.

Twists shift runners out of a forwards-only plane, releasing built-up tension in the muscles in the side of the torso, hips and legs. While some of yoga's rotations require a little effort, this simple pose is about letting go. Ensure your legs are relaxed and not hovering above the floor by propping your knees with cushions.

Lie down and draw your legs into your abdomen. If your back is stiff begin instead with your legs bent and feet hip-distance apart and resting on the floor. Press your lower back into the floor and take your arms out shoulder-height,

palms face up. As you breathe out lower your knees down to the floor on the right side and turn your head to your left. Repeat on the other side.

WIDE-LEGGED TWIST

Wide-legged twist stretches glute medius, the iliotibial band, torso, back and shoulders.

For a relaxed twist variation that targets the outer hip and iliotibial band try taking your feet wide. The deeper version of this pose is a good remedy for tight outer hips and IT band.

Lie on your back with your arms out shoulder-

height, palms face up. Bend your legs and heel/toe your feet out wider. As you breathe out lower your knees down to the floor on your right side and turn your head to the left. For a deeper stretch lift your right leg off the floor and place your right heel on top of your left knee. The extra weight will draw both legs down into a more intense stretch.

Overtraining: symptoms

Distance runners can be particularly susceptible to overtraining, or 'unexplained underperformance syndrome' as it is also known. But how can you recognise the signs? Here are ten of them:

1 Heavy, leaden legs
2 Irritability or mood swings
3 A psychological dependence on your next 'runner's high'
4 Frequent colds or upper respiratory infections
5 Insomnia or poor quality sleep
6 Lack of sex drive
7 Loss of enthusiasm for running
8 Lack of improvement, or decrease, in performance
9 An increase in common running injuries
10 An inability to concentrate.

Overtraining: prevention

So you know what overtraining is – now what can you do to avoid it? Here are five suggestions:

1 Schedule at least one rest day a week
2 Take a total break annually for a week or month
3 Swap a run for a yoga class
4 Cross train by cycling or swimming
5 Alternate light and heavy runs.

RELAXED SIDE-BEND

Relaxed side-bend stretches the whole of the side of the body, including the iliotibial band, glute medius and the obliques.

This posture – sometimes called banana pose – is a lying version of the standing iliotibial band stretch. But the benefits can be felt higher up in the side of the hips and torso. After students have held the posture for a minute I sometimes come round and move their feet a bit further round so the body adopts a more curved position.

Lie down. Sweep your arms up and interlace your fingers. Move your arms, head and legs over to your right so your body curves. To go deeper into the side-bend cross your left foot over your right at the ankle. Close your eyes.

Lower back releasers

If you suffer from tightness or a dull ache in your lower back region after running try releasing tension with the following simple movements.

LOW BACK MASSAGE

Lie on your back and slowly draw your legs into your abdomen. Keep the back of your head on the floor, but if your head tilts back, place a cushion or block underneath it. Rock from side to side. To massage higher, in your mid-back, hug your legs in tighter and lift your head towards your legs. To shift the emphasis to the sacrum keep your knees together but move your legs further away until your arms straighten. Work in circles around your sacrum.

LOW BACK RELEASER

Keep your left leg hugged into your abdomen and slide your right leg down along the floor. Point your left toes to the ceiling and press the back of your right knee into the mat. Slowly rotate your left foot. Stay for five slow breaths then switch sides.

CHILD

Another forward-bend made for winding down. Place some yoga blocks or cushions under your forehead if it doesn't touch the floor. Child requires good flexion in your knees, so if you find kneeling uncomfortable try tortoise instead. Or try a wide-legged child by taking your knees to the edge of the mat, toes together and sinking back on your heels.

Come to all fours. Breathe in. As you breathe out sit slowly back on your heels and rest your

forehead on the floor (or on a few blocks/ cushions). Relax your arms by your sides, palms face upwards.

EXTENDED CHILD

Extended child is ideal and provides a welcome back and shoulder stretch after a long run. Come to all fours. As you breathe out sit slowly back on your heels. Extend both arms out in front and press your palms into the floor. For a deeper feeling of spinal decompression, inch your fingertips forwards and draw your hips back, in the opposite direction.

Leg recovery

Literally taking the weight off your feet feels fantastic after a long run. Yoga has many 'inversions', from simply elevating the legs on a chair, to a full shoulder stand that will drain the fluid that accumulates in the lower body through running. These variations are ideal post-run as they are simple and require little energy. Inversions also calm the nervous system ready for deeper relaxation, meditation or sleep.

LEGS ON A CHAIR

If you are lacking wall space, simply lie close to a chair and rest your calves on the surface so your legs are at a right angle. Draw your chin downwards, resting your head on a cushion if your chin pokes upwards.

LEGS UP THE WALL

Shuffle close to the wall and turn side-on to it. Lie down and slide your legs up the wall so your heels rest on its surface. Move further away if the hamstring stretch is too intense. Draw your chin downwards. Place a cushion or block under your head if your chin pokes upwards. Move your arms away from your body and turn your palms face upwards to open your chest or rest your palms on your abdomen and focus on the slow rise and fall of your belly.

To vary the position:

1 Bring the soles of your feet together.

2 Straighten your legs and spread them wide.

3 Perform a glute stretch by moving further away from the wall, bending your left leg and placing your ankle on top of your right thigh (or higher). Flex your left foot.

STRAP INVERSION

To both invert your legs and stretch your hamstrings, lie down, loop a strap around the balls of your feet and straighten your legs. Walk your hands up the strap until your arms are straight, and draw your chin downwards. If you feel your legs are tipping forwards and you are struggling to hold them at a 90° angle, opt for legs up the wall or legs on a chair to avoid unnecessarily stressing your hip flexors.

BREATHING TO RELAX

The way that you breathe can have dramatic mood-altering effects. Some yoga breathing techniques are uplifting and energising. The following three have a soporific effect making them ideal for winding down or taking the edge off nerves before a race.

BASIC NOSTRIL BREATHING

The nostril breathing techniques rapidly calm the mind and level the emotions. Try the basic technique before moving onto the alternate nostril breathing. Practise before bed, or to get back to sleep if you wake in the middle of the night.

Raise the right hand up close to the face. Curl the three middle fingers into the palm so just the little finger and thumb are extended. Sit tall and close your eyes.

- **Step 1:** Inhale through both nostrils
- **Step 2:** Close your right nostril and release a long, slow exhalation through your left.
- **Step 3:** Inhale through both nostrils
- **Step 4:** Close your left nostril and release a long, slow exhalation through your right.
- **Step 5:** Continue, moving from side to side.
- **Step 6:** Lower your hand down to your lap and breathe in and out through both nostrils, focusing on the flow of air.

ALTERNATE NOSTRIL BREATHING

- **Step 1:** Close your left nostril and take a long, slow inhalation through your right.
- **Step 2:** Close your right nostril and release a long, slow exhalation through your left.
- **Step 3:** Inhale left. Close your left nostril and exhale right.
- **Step 4:** Continue, moving from side to side.
- **Step 5:** Lower your hand down to your lap and breathe through both nostrils, focusing on the flow of air.

OCEAN BREATH

The Sanskrit name for this technique is ujjayi, but it is sometimes named 'ocean breath' so that students can connect with the soft wave-like sound it produces in the throat. The idea is to partially constrict your throat to make an audible soothing sound. This sound is not forced and only heard by you (think soft waves lapping, not huge waves crashing).

- **Step 1:** Imagine you are close to a mirror and want to fog it up with your exhalation. Breathe in through your nose, open your mouth and exhale, listening to the soft hissing sound.
- **Step 2:** Now repeat the process but keep your mouth closed throughout. You should hear a similar, but quieter sound.
- **Step 3:** Close your eyes and continue, refining the sound and pressure on your throat and channelling all your attention onto the sound.

RELAXATION

Relaxation in yoga is called *yoga nidra*, which translates as 'yoga sleep'. However, rather than drifting off into an unconscious sleep state a good yoga relaxation teaches you how to consciously relax. Once learnt, these relaxation techniques can be used to unwind your body after a late training session or to calm your mind after a hectic day at work. They also prime both body and mind for restorative, deep sleep – essential for repairing muscle damage caused by running.

THE PHYSIOLOGY OF RELAXATION

Relaxation is simply a process of encouraging our parasympathetic nervous system to function. It is the polar opposite of the highly aroused state we feel when stressed or on high alert (blood pumping, heart racing…). During relaxation the sympathetic 'fight or flight' response is subdued.

Physiological responses to relaxation include the following:

- respiration decreases
- heart rate decreases
- metabolism slows
- digestion increases.

Savasana: pose of relaxation

Savasana is designed for optimum muscular release. The ideal relaxed state is one of alert restfulness. The body is relaxed enough to release tension. The mind is calm but not dull and sleepy. Prepare for relaxation by lying in savasana as described below, and roll your head from side to side in slow motion. Take four or five deep abdominal breaths, or 'sigh out' your breath by inhaling deeply through your nose, opening your mouth and releasing an audible sigh.

Ensure the following:

- **You are warm:** Your body temperature will lower as your heart slows, so put on layers and socks or use a light blanket.
- **You are comfortable:** Bend your legs and place your feet on the floor if your lower back is uncomfortable with your legs extended.
- **You won't be disturbed:** Switch off your phone and allow yourself ten minutes of uninterrupted peace and quiet.

Yoga relaxation is mainly done lying on a rug or yoga mat on the floor, but the instructions below can be adapted to a sitting posture.

- **Head:** Roll your head from side to side, then back to the centre. Draw your chin slightly downwards to lengthen the back of your neck. If your chin points upwards, place a cushion under your head.
- **Face:** Close your eyes and soften your eye muscles, relax your jaw and let your tongue rest in your mouth.
- **Breathing:** Breathe through your nose. Let your breathing fall into a natural rhythm as if you were sleeping.
- **Shoulders:** Let your shoulders become heavy and relax onto the mat.
- **Arms:** Move your arms away from the sides of your body.
- **Hands:** Turn your palms up to open your shoulders. Let your fingers curl.
- **Abdomen:** Relax your abdomen and let it rise and fall naturally.
- **Legs:** Let the full weight of your legs relax onto the mat.
- **Feet:** Let your feet fall out to the sides.

Obstacles to relaxation

1 **Fidgeting and twitching:** The instruction to 'lie still' can create the urge to fidget in many beginners who find they have a twitchy leg or an itchy nose that must be scratched. This is normal; we are unaccustomed to lying still unless sleeping. Perform some static stretches or restorative yoga postures from this chapter and take some slow deep breaths with your eyes closed before lying down.

2 **Constant mental distractions:** As soon as your body is relaxed your mind can whir into action; running through the day's activities or planning future events. Again, this is perfectly normal and will take patience to tackle. Just being aware that your mind is drifting is half the battle. Keep drawing your wandering attention back, either to the soft ebb and flow of your breath or to a fixed physical point like the space between your eyebrows.

3 **Falling asleep:** The aim of relaxation is to learn how to consciously relax. When you sleep you are unconscious and therefore oblivious to your body or mind. If sleepy anchor your attention to your breathing.

The benefits of massage

Massage shares many stress-relieving benefits with yoga relaxation. It lowers the blood pressure and provides a chance to rest body and mind. Massage is also said to increase circulation by pushing lactic acid and metabolic waste out of the muscles although its exact benefits are still debated.

A regular rub-down will, at the very least, provide an opportunity to tune into your body. Your massage therapist can pinpoint any areas with tightness or adhesions that may be susceptible to injury.

Pick your massage time carefully though, as it can temporarily cause your legs to feel heavy; not something you want just before a big run or race. There are, of course, cheaper alternatives to a massage therapist, as long as you have no specific injuries that require a professional's expert touch. All you need is a tennis ball and foam roller (firm foam log-shaped massage device around six inches in diameter). To self-massage the soles of your feet, stand up, place your foot onto the ball and gently roll up and down. A golf ball can provide a deeper, more intense massage

for the soles of the feet. A physiotherapist can advise on exactly how to use one to relieve plantar fasciitis (inflammation of the connective tissue on the soles of the feet.)

A foam roller is an effective way to self-massage your legs if you can handle the pain it can often reach the knots that stretching alone cannot. Place the roller just above your knee and lie on it, working upwards in strokes to break down tight quad muscles. Flip over to work into your hamstrings and lower into your calves and Achilles. Shift onto your side with the roller under your thigh, and move up and down the length of your iliotibial band from just above your knee to the top of your thigh.

Finally, squat on the roller (or a plastic spikey massage ball) so that it nestles in the middle of the glutes, and move in a small circular motion to massage your glutes and piriformis.

Relaxation 1: Tense and release

This simple, systematic relaxation is great for runners with twitchy legs or those without the patience to lie still. It works on the principle that if a muscle is tightly contracted for a few seconds, it relaxes further when you release the hold.

Take four slow breaths through your nose.

1 **Feet:** Inhale. Flex your feet so your toes point up to the ceiling and your heels push forwards. Hold, then exhale and relax. Let your feet fall out to the sides.

2 **Legs:** Inhale. Press the backs of your knees into the floor/bed, engaging your leg muscles. Hold. As you exhale let your legs relax and become heavy.

3 **Buttocks:** Inhale. Clench your buttocks and hold. Exhale and soften.

4 **Abdomen:** Inhale. Press your belly button into the floor/bed. Pause and then exhale and relax your abdomen.

5 **Chest:** Inhale. Arch your back, lifting your sternum to the ceiling. Hold. Exhale and release.

6 **Neck:** Inhale. Raise your head off the floor and draw in your chin. Pause. Exhale and lower your head back down. Roll your head slowly from side to side.

7 **Arms and hands:** Inhale. Lock your elbows and make fists with your hands. Hold. Release on the out-breath.

8 **Face and jaw:** Inhale. Screw up the muscles of your face and clench your teeth. Pause. Exhale and soften.

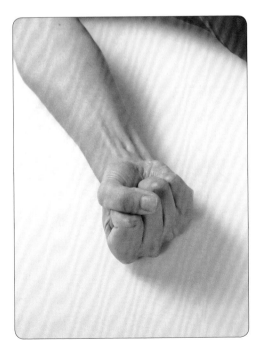
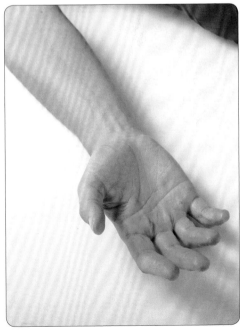

Relaxation 2: Heavy body

Combine mental imagery with your breathing to create a sensation of physical heaviness. If your legs feel particularly fidgety after running spend more time on them, creating a feeling of 'lead legs'.

Repeat steps 1–8 of the tense and release relaxation, but this time concentrate on feelings of heaviness in each part of your body. For example, fix your attention on your head. Let the full weight of your heavy head sink into your pillow. Tell yourself about your 'heavy arms and leaden legs' pressing into the bed. Once you've worked from toes to head, it's important not to move as it breaks the 'spell' of heaviness, but if this happens, simply start again.

Relaxation 3: White light

Use this visualisation to expel any negative feelings or conflicts from your day.

Sit with a straight back, or lie in savasana. Imagine your body as totally transparent, as if made of glass. As you breathe in through your nose visualise pure white light flowing into your head, neck and shoulders. As you breathe out imagine the exhalation is a dark smoky grey. Breathe in white light into your whole torso and down the length of your arms. Breathe out grey, but a little lighter in colour. Breathe white light into your legs, picturing it flowing down to your knees, ankles and feet. Breathe out a very light grey exhalation. Finally breathe white light into your whole body and breathe out white light. End by visualising your whole body swirling with white light.

Relaxation 4: Sitting relaxation

Sometimes it's not possible to lie flat. This sitting relaxation can be done anywhere and has the added benefit of releasing tension in your neck and upper back.

Sit in an upright but comfortable position, either cross-legged, kneeling or on a chair. Lengthen your spine and release your shoulders down away from your ears. Close your eyes. Keeping your back straight, allow your head to drop slowly forwards. Let your chin dip into your throat. Feel the back of your neck stretching and lengthening. Continue to let your head curl down. Let it round your shoulders and upper back. Feel your spine curving further until your mid-back rounds. Let your head descend until it reaches a natural stop. Pause here with your back rounded and breathe slowly. Now reverse the process – again in stages. Begin to uncurl from the base of your spine. Gradually straighten your lower, mid- and upper spine, feeling your vertebrae slotting back into place. Keep your chin tucked into your throat until your neck vertebrae straighten, then slowly raise your head. Sit for a moment. Then open your eyes.

CALMING MEDITATION

A negative mindset, brought on by life's stresses, can impact many aspects of training, from diet to quality of sleep. While yoga relaxation encompasses the whole body, meditation narrows in on the activities of the mind. We have already explored some aspects of meditation that can be done while running in Chapter 10. The following exercises are designed purely to calm and clear the mind, although the more proficient you become at home-based meditation, the easier it will be to control the mind on the run.

HOW TO SIT

Traditionally, a cross-legged or lotus position provides the wide, stable base required for meditation, accompanied by a long, straight back. However, if sitting crossed-legged is uncomfortable or painful either prop the position by placing cushions under your knees and leaning against a wall or sit on a chair with your feet firmly planted on the floor.

Meditation 1: Listening

This listening technique is a method of drawing the focus inwards, stage by stage. It requires a quiet location. Sit and listen in each stage for thirty seconds to a minute.

1 Listen to far away sounds. This might be the low rumble of traffic or plane engine noise.

2 Listen to noises just outside the building – maybe a passing car or a bird singing.

3 Listen to sounds inside the room or building – perhaps the air conditioning or heating.

4 Listen for the very quiet sound of your own breathing. Remain here for as long as you are comfortable, listening to, and observing, your breath.

Meditation 2: Labelling thoughts

Our thoughts usually fall into two main categories: thinking about the past and worrying about the future. This technique systematically 'labels' thoughts as they arise, thereby gaining control over them.

Sit comfortably with a straight back and start to focus on the flow of breath through your nose. Take five to ten breaths just allowing your mind to settle. Now notice every time your mind jumps into the future or draws back to the past. Label these thoughts as 'past' or 'future', and forget about them. If this proves difficult, simply say the thought aloud ('bills' or 'meeting tomorrow').

Commuter meditation

The best time to meditate in an ideal world is before breakfast, but for those with small children, or a very early start it just isn't feasible. Instead try meditating on the train. The other commuters will assume you are napping and the distractions of the train carriage will provide an extra challenge. If you can meditate here, with the noise and movement, be assured that you can calm and control the mind anywhere – in a stressful work situation or sitting in the car half an hour before a race. Start every meditation with a few moments of slow breathing through your nose. Either stick with this simple 'breath-watching'

meditation, drawing your mind back to your nostrils every time it wanders, or select one of the meditations offered in this chapter.

INDEX